HEAVEN AND NATURE SING

an advent devotional

Connie Armerding | Donna Dahlstrom | Jan Cowles
Jodi Cowles | Bethany McMillon | Hollis Mitchell
Rachael Mitchell | Indee Musa | Leslee Stewart

Requests for information should be addressed to:
The Unknown Authors Club
P.O. Box 170397
Boise, Idaho 83717
www.theunknownauthorsclub.com

Softcover ISBN: 979-8-9868277-6-6
eBook: 979-8-9868277-7-3

Edited and Compiled by: Jodi Cowles, Paige Elliott, Rachael Mitchell, Leslee Stewart
Cover design: Leslee Stewart
Interior design: Rachel Langaker

Printed in the United States of America.

CONTENTS

WHAT IS ADVENT?

When I think of advent, I most often think of the 400 years of waiting between the Old Testament and the New; between the promise and the fulfillment; between the last word from God in heaven, and the birth of His Son, Jesus—the promised and long-awaited Messiah.

Advent in its most simple form is a period of waiting—the four Sundays before Christmas Day—but it's a robust waiting as opposed to a passive one. Strenuously believing. Vigorously hoping. Agonizingly trusting. Yes, those verbs all have *-ing* endings, meaning continuous action, not a one and done deed.

And what is the focal point of that belief, that hope, that trust? What is the engine that powers the *-ing* continuous action over sometimes hundreds of years? Most certainly not the circumstances in which we live, the evil before our eyes, the lies shouted all around—*He's never coming. He's not going to fix this. He won't come through.* Not even the promise itself can be the focal point, but only the One who made the promise.

But if God is completely worthy of trust, if He does not lie, if His purposes are always accomplished, we can continue to wait—robustly. And what you will find in the following pages are the words of women with the knowledge, the lived experience, and the certainty to testify that not a single promise from God will stand unfulfilled. No matter how long it takes.

In these four Sundays prior to Christmas Day, we welcome you to wait with us, to prepare for His coming, to cheer His arrival. Let us wait, with sure hope, together.

— **Jodi Cowles**

HOW TO USE THIS DEVOTIONAL

This book was written to be an evergreen Advent devotional, meaning you can read it year after year. It is divided into four weeks, with each week consisting of one short devotional to read Monday through Saturday, followed by a group devotional time on Sunday (which can also be done individually).

When to Start

To follow the plan, we suggest you <u>begin Week One on the Monday prior to the first Sunday in December</u>. Depending on the year, this might mean you will begin the devotionals during the last week of November. Following this model will allow you to be in sync with Advent no matter when the dates might fall year to year.

Candles for Sunday Devotional

Each week during the Sunday devotional, you will be lighting an Advent candle. Candles can be arranged traditionally or non-traditionally, whichever you prefer.

For a traditional arrangement you will need:

- An advent wreath or greenery
- A candelabra/candle holders

- Three purple candles for weeks 1-3
- One pink candle for week 4
- One larger white candle in the center for Christmas Day

For a non-traditional arrangement you will need:

- Any candle will do
- Add one candle each week leading up to Christmas Day

Bonus Content

The book also includes a recommended set of scriptures to read on Christmas Day and a bonus chapter about Epiphany.

HEAVEN

One would expect heaven to announce its arrival with a super-sized brass band leading a parade, complete with elephants, fireworks, and a grand finale of a Zeus-like, god-man standing in a gold convertible and smiling, waving, and tossing dollar bills to the crowd.

But heaven breaking through to earth happened in obscurity. Some shepherds got a terrifyingly dazzling show, but they hardly seemed like the right audience to broadcast important news. Heaven wasn't looking for a grand show as its original point of entry and still quietly resides on earth in the hearts of God's people.

Preparing for the arrival of heaven in this season doesn't happen in the hustle and bustle of the holiday, but in the quiet contemplation of one's heart.

HEAVEN

week 1 – monday

But Mary treasured all these things and
pondered them in her heart.
Luke 2:19

Christmas-green garlands and red bows hang merrily on each pew lining the center aisle. An evergreen tree stretches tall, reaching toward the apex of the church ceiling. Overhead chandelier lights cast an especially warm glow through the sanctuary. I stand, close to the back, and hold my husband's hand as the organ music swells with Christmas song.

My cranberry-red sweater stretches taut across my growing belly. I place my other hand just below my ribs and rub where I felt the last kick. We can be found in this row almost every week to worship and learn. As we sit following the worship songs and preparing for the lesson, I scoot close, and his arm wraps lightly around my shoulders. Our anniversary is approaching; the newness of our marriage is not lost on me, nor is the comfort I feel with his presence beside me. I steal a glance his way, and he pats my shoulder.

I reach for my Bible to open to today's passage, but my thoughts wander to Mary, centuries ago. Pregnant at Christmas. Preparing to bring Heaven to earth. Did the kicks of King Jesus land just below her ribs? Did He somersault in the womb as music swelled? Though they had not come together in marriage, did she find comfort in the strong hands of Joseph as he supported and helped her along the trek to Bethlehem? Scripture tells us she treasured all these things and pondered them in her heart. I, too, tuck the memory of this almost-Christmas moment into my heart, burying its treasure deep.

Months later, I sit in the same sanctuary, but this time with a wiggly little blonde boy in my lap. The church hasn't yet been decorated for Christmas, but families are packed in for the "dedication service" tradition. The music rises and our boy begins to bounce in my lap. A video plays on the screen showing pictures of each child ready for dedication and flashes the Bible verse chosen for them by their parents. He snuggles into my shoulder and wraps his little arms around my neck; I pat his back in rhythm to the music and scoot close to his dad. A moment later, our son's picture flashes on the screen along with the Bible verse, Luke 2:40, *And the child grew and became strong; he was filled with wisdom and the grace of God was upon him.*

As the video closes, we rise and walk toward the altar of the church. The pastor prays over us. My husband and I stand together, one of his hands resting on my waist, the other on our son's back. We pray. For just a moment, time seems to pause. I gather the details of the moment and fold them into my memories and heart.

Repeatedly, in the coming years, a version of this scene repeats, and my heart remembers. The two of us watch as our son plays in the sandbox on a sunny day. He pushes the dump truck through the sand, fills it, dumps it, and repeats along a different sandbox path, constantly jabbering as he plays. We celebrate as he chooses to give his life to the Lord and is baptized at church. We cheer him on from the sidelines in a football game. I watch for his number amid the pile of linemen, screaming and stomping in the stands for big hits and high-fiving my husband when our team scores. We pray over him when he encounters difficulty. I trust, through hardships, he is growing into the man the Lord has designed him to be. My heart breaks in some moments and soars in others. But in each, I tuck the memory into my core and ponder the gift the Lord has given me to be his mom.

As readers of Scripture, we don't know much about Jesus' life as a boy, except the stories in Matthew 2 and Luke 2. We know of his birth in Bethlehem, the worship of the shepherds and the praise of the host of angels, his presentation and consecration at the temple, the family's flight to Egypt, trips to Jerusalem for Passover, and his childhood teaching at the temple, which caused Mary and Joseph panic. But between these extraordinary stories were undoubtedly many unrecorded and ordinary moments in which Jesus grew, and in which Mary pondered and marveled at the Gift of Heaven.

— **Bethany McMillon**

Reflect & Respond

In today's fast-paced life, we fill the Christmas season with merriment and festivities, gifts, and celebrations. As you begin this Advent season, start by pausing and asking yourself these questions:

What am I pondering?

How will I treasure the Gift of Heaven in this season?

HEAVEN

week 1 - tuesday

The heavens declare the glory of God; the skies proclaim
the work of his hands. Day after day they pour forth speech;
night after night they reveal knowledge.
Psalm 19:1-2

Beautifully haunting lyrics spurred on by the strings of a lonely guitar wafted out into the darkness. I took inventory of the women sitting quietly nearby, scattered around a makeshift fire pit, most of whom I did not know. The breeze, grazing gently over nearby blades of grass and rustling through the encampment, had a bite to it. I was acutely aware of the sounds around me – crackling from the dwindling fire, the softly lapping waves over the lake before us, and even the howling of coyotes far off in the distance, from between the trees.

Most palpable of all, though, was the lack of people noise. No one bustled around, stood up, or spoke to their neighbor. Everyone seemed as mesmerized by the guitarist's lyrics as I was. Outside of her gentle voice and the soft humming of the guitar, I was enveloped in stillness. The kind of stillness you wish for when children are running around, or teenagers are slamming doors and your pile of work and endless conference calls seem to stream out into infinity. This was a stillness found in the night at a country ranch, far from the chaos of an ever-growing city. Beautiful stillness.

As I wrapped my sweater tightly around me, it suddenly occurred to me to look up. How often are we, busy humans, in an environment and atmosphere where we can experience stillness long enough to look around, about, and up at our surroundings? I marveled at how, even at night, the sky held a patchwork of magnificent colors—an obsidian black intertwined with varying degrees of inky blue, gray, and a milky white that seemed to pour into the darkness like creamer from an almost full moon.

I was in awe. The Hebrew word translated into 'awe' in scripture is *yirah*. It represents the fear of the Lord but also means respect, reverence, and worship. In that moment I felt the magnitude of my reverence and worship for a God who created such precise and purposeful beauty.

I couldn't take my eyes off the landscape above. Stars dotted the clear night sky like glimmering crystals all around, varying in size, brightness, and distance. I felt embraced by the heavenly realms, and unconsciously I lifted a hand as if to attempt to touch them. "What bright, clear stars," I thought as I realized I hadn't seen them in a city sky in many years. It suddenly occurred to me that the stars I was looking at *right then* were the same stars that existed in the sky from the moment God placed them there. The *exact* same stars that guided the Israelites in their 40-year Exodus through the wilderness. The *exact* same stars that dotted the night sky when a young virgin girl and her confused fiancée rode into Bethlehem to be counted. These were the *exact* same stars that brought heaven itself down to earth in the form of a precious Middle Eastern infant who would change the world. These *exact* same stars dotted the heavens around 5 or 6 B.C., when the Magi would travel, from distant lands to the hometown of a two-year-old toddler to celebrate and worship the future Savior of the world.

How did God use the stars to point the Magi to Jesus? How did He cause them to brighten and move so that the wise men could navigate by them? While we don't know the answers to these questions and many others, there is astronomical and historical evidence suggesting that the Star of Bethlehem was a comet, visible in 5 B.C. and also described in ancient Chinese records. In 1991, the Quarterly Journal of the Royal Astronomical Society wrote that this comet fits Matthew's biblical description of a star that newly appeared, traveled slowly through the sky against the star background, and 'stood over' Bethlehem. They believed that there could be evidence that the triple conjunction of Saturn and Jupiter in 7 B.C., the massing of Saturn, Jupiter, and Mars in 6 B.C., and finally the appearance in 5 B.C. of the star of Bethlehem would have been rich in significance to the Magi, and the combination could have provided an obvious sign that a mighty new king was about to be born in Bethlehem.

Though there is lots of compelling evidence to bring us closer to the infant who became our resurrected King, we will never know the full story, until one day, sitting at the feet of Jesus, we learn all the truths of heaven. For now, go somewhere quiet, look up into the sky and around you, at your surroundings—the sunrise and sunset, the birds flitting from tree to tree, the grass growing upward like it was asked to, the smell of the flowers, the stillness of night, and the quiet of dawn—and heaven will feel very close indeed.

— **Indee Musa**

Reflect & Respond

Go outside with your family this Christmas season. Take a nature walk or gather everyone into the backyard or on the front porch. Quietly take in the surroundings for a few minutes. What do you see around you that makes you marvel at our Creator? Discuss the things that can be seen or unseen by each family member that point to a marvelous God.

week 1 – wednesday

When I consider your heavens,
the work of your fingers,
the moon and the stars,
which you have set in place,
what is mankind that you are mindful of them,
human beings that you care for them?
You have made them a little lower than the angels
and crowned them with glory and honor.
Psalm 8:3–5

My Sunday school teacher posed the question, "What do you imagine heaven will be like?" to a wiggly bunch of eager 5-year-olds. She placed a few baskets of worn-out crayons around the table with white paper and instructed us to draw our answers. As a child of furious creativity and action, I pondered the assignment for a brief second, but already knew exactly what my answer would look like. My lips pursed tightly in concentration and my crayons revealed in full color my best vision of a future promise: a long table with a bearded Jesus at one end and me at the other. We have oddly shaped arms that resemble round logs with five hotdog-shaped fingers each. We both have half smiles plastered on our faces, a new-to-me clever technique I copied from a friend to show Jesus and me smiling at each other. We're happy to see each other, but we're mostly smiling because in the middle of the table, for us to share, is a giant bowl of conversation hearts. In my candy-deprived childhood, my theology of heaven consisted of giant bowls of chalk-like hearts to eat with Jesus.

Though conversation hearts are no longer my first choice of candy as an adult, my theology of heaven hasn't changed much: I hope Jesus and I can sit at a table or on a fluffy patch of grass, eat some candy, and chat.

As a child I only had my imagination and slivers of information from my parents and Sunday school teacher, to construct a picture of heaven: "The streets are made out of gold!" "There are no tears in heaven!" "Your grandma is sliding down rainbows in heaven!" My imagination filled in the rest, complete with some Willy Wonka additions. Until I pass from this physical dimension into the dimension of being fully alive and face-to-face with Christ, I won't know if my imagination has led me to truth or astray in regards to heaven. However, even as an adult, I'm confident it's only through imagination we are able to consider and wonder about the unknown, and sometimes unlock a deeper understanding that reason alone could never contend with. When thinking about heaven, imagination is a requirement. Not because heaven is an imaginary fairyland in a world of make-believe, but because these rational bodies which depend so deeply on matter, proof, and reason need the imagination to punch through what is rational to imagine heaven's fantastical reality, far beyond our wildest dreams.

But "imagination" for many means "pretend." It's how we can watch—and enjoy—movies like *The Incredibles*, Marvel movies, or *The Cat in the Hat*. They're fun and fantastical and would be crazy and terrifying if anything in those movies ever happened in real life. But that type of imaginative pretend is different from engaging my imagination regarding heaven because I'm convinced heaven isn't pretend. Heaven is what we've all been waiting for, the fully alive, greatest reality we can't wait to be a part of. But since the reality of heaven doesn't yet perpetually exist on earth, I need help holding onto the hope of it until it does.

Jesus tapped into the imagination of his friends as a teaching tool throughout the four Gospels. Luke 11:5 is one example. He sparks the imagination: *"Suppose you have a friend, and you go to him at midnight..."* Before he gets to the meat of his lesson he's engaging the imagination of his friends to ask them to "suppose" two things: 1) you have a friend and 2) you're attempting to engage with this friend at midnight. Jesus captivates the imagination to set up an interesting story. In short, Jesus shows rather than tells, using the imagination to unlock his illustrations.

Contemplative spiritual exercises created and used for centuries by Christian mystics connect and engage the heart, mind, and imagination through centering prayer, scriptural contemplation or *lectio divina,* breath prayers, and other practices. Contemplation is "the practice of being fully present—in heart, mind, and body—to what is in a way that allows you to creatively respond and work toward what could be."[1] The anonymous author of *The Cloud of Unknowing,* a contemplative devotional written in England during the last half of the fourteenth century, recommends a specific way of not-knowing:

---

1. "What Is Contemplation?," Center for Action and Contemplation, accessed July 12, 2023, https://cac.org/about/what-is-contemplation/.

"Knowledge hinders, not helps you in contemplation. Be content feeling moved in a delightful, loving way by something mysterious and unknown, leaving you focused entirely on God, with no other thought than of him alone."[2] Could the mind via the imagination, content with knowing and controlling less, actually be more in tune with the heart of God?

C.S. Lewis argued in *Selected Literary Essays* that "reason is the natural organ of truth… imagination is the organ of meaning." As a determined atheist as a young man, imagination was the key that unlocked the relationship between reason and faith. Thankfully, further along in his journey, imagination became the vehicle to communicate deep spiritual meaning through his stories in his *Narnia Chronicles*. Children and adults enjoy the adventure, fantastical creatures, and battle between good and evil as well as the deeper, layered spiritual truths contained in them. Spiritual truths become more personal, more colorful, richer, and more thoughtful when the imagination is engaged.

Similarly, Madeline L'Engle, in her triumphant book for artists and creators *Walking on Water,* beautifully affirms, "We live under the illusion that if we can acquire complete control, we can understand God… But the only way we can brush against the hem of our Lord or hope to be part of the creative process, is to have the courage, the faith, to abandon control."[3] It is imperative that even as we plod through the difficulties of this life our imaginations remain unhindered. Without them, we dwell too solidly here on earth living as though this is all there is—forgetting that the beauty, mystery, and goodness of heaven are barely invisible. Logic, reason, and absolutes

---

2. Anonymous, *The Cloud of Unknowing* (Boulder: Shambhala Publications, Inc., 2009), XXI.

3. Madeline L'Engle, *Walking on Water: Reflections on Faith and Art* (Colorado Springs: WaterBrook Press, 2014), 191.

remove the wonder from heaven, whereas imagination creates vision, wonder, and a childlike belief in that which we cannot see with our physical eyes. Imagination forms a wild hint of what could be.

Though I am more and more confident that conversation hearts will be the last candy allowed into heaven, (in fact they might be on the dessert menu in hell) giving my imagination permission to consider, to wander, to roam allows my heart to engage with otherworldly ideas and concepts too fantastical to be tethered to a rational earth.

— **Rachael Mitchell**

Reflect & Respond

Today, practice a contemplative prayer.

1. Choose a sacred word as a symbol of agreement with God's presence and movement within.

2. Sit comfortably with your eyes closed. Gently introduce the word to the space.

3. If your thoughts begin to wander, gently draw them back to the sacred word you have chosen.

4. At the end of the prayer time, remain in silence with your eyes closed for a few additional minutes.

HEAVEN

week 1 – thursday

*Be kind to one another, tenderhearted, forgiving
one another, as God in Christ forgave you.*
Ephesians 4:32 (ESV)

Consider the life cycle of an ice crystal descending from the heavens. Having attached itself to a particle of dust or salt, gravity pulls it to the earth's surface where, depending upon its location, it may melt into liquid before eventually rising as a vapor to form clouds in the sky above. The crystal will then find a different particle for another ride to earth. This cycle has been going on since the beginning of time. Falling and rising. Falling and rising. In the midst of those cycles, the liquid form we know as water provides saturation and healing to the parched earth below with its life-giving nutrients. Trees, insects, grass, animals, microorganisms, and humans alike all need the liquid form of ice crystals. Water. Is. Life.

Much to my delight, I have the privilege of living in a place that receives an average of 400 inches of snow each year, so I've grown quite familiar with the falling and rising of water molecules in their many forms. I've found that wind and temperature have everything to do with the shape and size of snowflakes. Many crystals can attach to one another on their descent to earth, creating large, fluffy snowflakes, while others might break apart as they collide with one another and feel like tiny grains of sugar. Many of our neighborhood snowflakes contribute to the construction of snow sculptures or line the path of an epic sledding hill. Some pack perfectly into snowballs while others are excellent canvases for snow angels. Many land in a nearby body of water and melt immediately. I have seen snowflakes grace the eyelashes of my giggling granddaughters or show off their perfect six points on jacket sleeves to the delight of a snowshoeing scout troop who took the time to notice. Some made it directly onto moist tongues as they danced their way through the air or dotted the windshields of passing cars.

Fortunately for all of us, the vast majority of snowflakes become part of deep snowpacks around the globe on various mountain peaks and ranges. I think of these locations as the precious caretakers of the fresh water that will soon be needed during the dry seasons. Some may be locked into a slow-moving glacier for many, many years, while others melt quickly with the lengthening days of spring. The warmth of the sun will eventually win by returning these combined snowflakes of the snowpack to their liquid state as drops of water. Drops gather into streams. Streams flow into rivers. Rivers wind their way into lakes or vast oceans. Along the way, water permeates the ground. It nourishes the vegetation. It quenches our thirst. It restores life. Water. Is. Life.

Just as the ice crystals fall to earth from above, heaven sent Jesus to earth for a season. During His time here, He permeated our culture by walking among us. Like melting snow, He nourished our souls with His examples of love and support for one another. He continues to quench our thirst for all that is good. When we drink in His goodness, we participate in restoring life to our hurting world through acts of kindness and generosity and compassion.

As a side note, I often struggle to understand scripture. My heart doesn't receive immediately, like frozen ground failing to instantly absorb moisture from snow. Occasionally I'll read a passage that resonates in the moment, and I absorb its instruction deep into my soul. But more often than not, I'll read a passage that just sits there, with no idea what it means or how to apply it to my life. Yet, over the years, something might thaw, either within me or within the scripture, and suddenly make sense. Sometimes the words from God fall like rain, easily absorbed, but other times they fall like snow that takes a season, or two or three, to melt into a form I understand. I take great comfort in Isaiah 55:10-11 (ESV): *"For as the rain and the snow come down from heaven and do not return there but water the earth, making it bring forth and sprout, giving seed to the sower and bread to the eater, so shall my word be that goes out from my mouth; it shall not return to me empty, but it shall accomplish that which I purpose, and shall succeed in the thing for which I sent it."* Eventually the passage will "accomplish" and "succeed" in communicating what God is trying to say. I just need to keep receiving it in whatever form it comes in.

Even though Jesus returned to heaven after His time on earth, similar to the way water droplets evaporate back into the atmosphere, His impact upon our lives on earth remains if we choose to follow His example of compassion, justice, empathy, and community. Every kind action, every word of encouragement, every helping hand is a way to satisfy a thirst for belonging. One snowflake may not seem significant, but millions of snowflakes together make a profound difference as they melt into a stream that flows into a river, then into a reservoir, and eventually out of a faucet. Every time I pour a glass of water or watch a snowflake drift from the sky, I am reminded of my own unique role in this continuous cycle that was modeled so beautifully by a young man who was born in a humble stable, walked on our earth, and showed me how to bless others with acts of kindness and compassion. And as the snowpack melts in the spring warmth, I am reminded that God's word will satisfy the thirst of my heart in its own time. And that satisfaction will multiply as I share acts of kindness with others.

— **Donna Dahlstrom**

Reflect & Respond

Reflect on a scripture passage that has "melted" slowly into your soul in the past, and consider how you will live differently today in light of this new understanding.

HEAVEN

week 1 - friday

*Because of God's tender mercy, the morning light
from heaven is about to break upon us, to give light
to those who sit in darkness and in the shadow of
death, and to guide us to the path of peace.*
Luke 1:78–79 (NLT)

Living in a neighborhood with a lot of cracks in the sidewalk, I've learned to keep a downward gaze as I make my daily trek around the block. As much as I'd prefer to keep my eyes focused on what's in front of me to avoid a car turning into a driveway or someone passing by on a bike, I am in greater danger of being injured by not keeping my eyes on the sidewalk. With its undulating levels, a walk around our block can be a hazard waiting to happen.

I should know. A few months ago while out on my daily jaunt, I was comfortably moving in my normal stride when I casually let my gaze drift up from the sidewalk. Suddenly, out of nowhere, a piece of sidewalk jumped up and tripped me, and I found my body falling forward. I hit the concrete sidewalk on one knee with a thud while the other crumbled beneath me. The force of my landing caused my upper body to then fall to my left and squarely smoosh my face in my neighbor's muddy front yard.

Dazed and confused over what had just happened, I slowly rolled onto my back, sat up, and started checking to make sure none of my bones were broken. While my bones were intact, my ego was not. The accident occurred at the busiest intersection in our neighborhood. As I looked around, I noticed there were four cars at the four-way stop. Immediately, my face went flush with embarrassment, as I imagined one of them probably had a dashboard camera, or maybe the neighbor had a Ring doorbell with new footage of me ungracefully kissing the earth. To this day, I'm confident they are replaying a clip of me falling over and over and over and over for friends when they visit.

Looking up can be hazardous. I like the control of keeping my gaze downward, focused on what's just ahead, watching out for cracks in the pavement that might cause me to stumble. But if I'm honest, I often treat my life like I treat my walk around the neighborhood. I am a master at trying to control everything and everyone around me in hopes of not getting caught off guard, not making a misstep, and not failing (or falling) miserably off course. It's smooth sailing when things go according to my carefully controlled plan. But when something unexpected pops up, much like the sidewalk crack on that fateful day, it can knock me off my feet and leave me spinning wildly out of control.

Looking up on my walk requires me to trust that the road I'm on won't fail me. I know the sidewalks around my neighborhood well enough to know that can be a dangerous gamble. Looking up requires me to trust the One who *makes [my] path straight."* (Proverbs

3:6) So often I say that I trust God, that I am committing my life into His more-than-capable hands, but the truth is, my walk betrays me. I think I know what is best, have a better path, and can control the outcome of my life if I just keep my head down and look out for cracks along the way.

The irony in all of this is that God looked down from Heaven and saw our need for a savior, someone we could place all our trust in, someone who could lead us *"...out of the kingdom of darkness and into the Kingdom of his dear Son, who purchased our freedom and forgave our sin."* (Col. 1:13-14)

In His mercy and love, He looked down from Heaven and sent Jesus. All He asks in return is for me to look up and surrender my whole life to Him. Looking up is the only way to experience His path of peace.

Which way will you choose to look today?

— **Leslee Stewart**

Reflect & Respond

Take a moment to go outside, stare up at the heavens, and be quiet and still for a few minutes. Then pray this prayer of surrender:

God, today I choose to look up. I look up to You once again and surrender my way, my will, and my life to You. Your plan is so much better than my plan. Forgive me for all the times I've doubted your goodness. Thank you for looking down on us and sending Jesus to be the light this world so desperately needed. I choose to allow His light to shine in my life and illuminate any darkness within me. As I lift my eyes to you, O God, enthroned in heaven, fill me with your peace today. Amen.

HEAVEN

week 1 - saturday

But very truly I tell you, it is for your good that I am going away. Unless I go away, the Advocate will not come to you; but if I go, I will send him to you.
John 16:7

Heaven is hard to grasp. It lives as an idea that is just out of my reach and challenging to wrap my mind around. If heaven is referenced as a "better place" than here on earth, why don't I feel that way? The older I get and the more death surrounds me, the more I long to grow in my understanding of heaven. And I wonder if I am not alone. Is heaven really better than here?

A few years beyond my college graduation, I lost someone I love, my dear friend, Andrew. He was killed in a head-on car crash. We spent our college years growing in friendship and pontificating about life, faith, and futures. We shared a core value: faith in Jesus. After Andrew passed, I did not doubt that he was in heaven. But, I didn't want him to be there. I wanted him to be here. I missed him.

And I was confronted with a belief I had not articulated until that moment. I thought *here* was better.

I felt conflicted when I thought of Andrew in heaven. I feared that it would be boring. Andrew was an artist with a sharp and witty mind. He was clever, with so much untapped creative genius. Would that go to waste?

This moment of crisis presented me with an opportunity to work out my wonky theology of heaven and sit with my questions. I had to own and confront my thoughts to see where they were faulty. My view of heaven needed a reframe, and the Advent season is helping me to see it.

Advent is a season of waiting. In the waiting, God's people encounter a surprise different than anyone could have imagined. Heaven came to earth in the form of a baby. It was a cosmic crash—an in-breaking of God's kingdom in a way no one could have predicted. This baby king is different and better than we think, with surprising twists and turns in how His arrival unfolds. Many devoutly religious people missed the unfolding of this heavenly drama because of their preconceived ideas. What they thought got in the way of what was real.

Heaven is not theoretical; it is literal. Descriptions of floating clouds and an endless choir in white robes are not helpful imagery. They steer our minds in the wrong direction. Heaven is more than we can fathom. In allowing the truth of Scripture to activate my imagination rather than the cultural stereotypes, I hold a hope-filled belief that heaven is better. I traded in the cheap, hollow depictions for something of substance.

In a season of waiting for things that are not yet as they should be, disillusionment and disappointment are familiar companions.

Remember that God has a history of showing up in the middle of our mess in new and unexpected ways, providing an outcome beyond our scope of possibility. Scripture repeatedly tells that story.

We need a heavenly reframe. The Advent story speaks of heaven coming to us. The arrival of a King born to a commoner is the backdrop for heaven's entrance. God came to be with us. Heaven is the answer to a relationship with God, extending for eternity. God came *to us* to pursue our hearts, to join us to his family. God meets us here on earth, the space we reside until He calls us home to heaven for eternity. Leaning on the truth of Scripture to guide me, I have come to realize that God, in His divine timing, called Andrew to his true home, the place where his creativity and wit will have their full potential realized. Heaven is the place God has prepared for us to be with Him forever. Heaven is our home. And home is where we long to be.

— **Connie Armerding**

Reflect & Respond

What images come to mind when you think of heaven? What notions do you have that need to be examined? Do you believe heaven is better than here? Explain.

Read and reflect on these Scripture passages. Let the truth of Scripture be what forms your mind and opinions on heaven as our home.

John 14: 1-3
Matthew 6: 19-20
John 11: 25-26
Philippians 3:20-21

HEAVEN

The first Sunday of Advent

On Sundays during Advent we encourage you to gather with family and friends to enjoy fellowship and a time of encountering God together during the holiday season. (The devotion can also be done individually.)

During your time, you will be reading a reflection poem, discussing a few questions, participating in an optional exercise, and ending the time by lighting the first Advent candle, singing a song, and reading scripture. Make sure everything is ready before you begin.

Ask someone to read the Reflection out loud:

> *what do they think up there in heaven*
> *as the moment's drawing near*
> *did You share with them Your plan*
> *did You speak and make it clear*
>
> *was it even possible for them*
> *to comprehend this plan*
> *where the God without constraint*
> *would come and dwell here, become Man*

all of those beings up in heaven
who have never broken "free"
the ones who swarm around Your throne
who sing and sing of Your holy

what do they think up there in heaven
as the moment's drawing near
as the star from deepest reaches
moves in closer, almost here

the one You lit a million years ago
and started on its way
it's been traveling all this time
to come to this appointed day

You who dwell in highest heaven
no other like You in consistence
yet highest heaven can't contain You
there's no end to Your existence

what do they think up there in heaven
as a girl draws near a stable
as a boy guides donkey, sure
so strange it looks to be a fable

are they trembling as they watch
wondering what You're about to do
for love of beings in rebellion
who rarely look above to You

from heaven vanished, nine long months
Emmanuel has left the room
the spark that lit up all creation
packed inside a tiny womb

what do they think up there in heaven
divine infinity descends
an endless pool without reserve
on Him the whole good plan depends

how can it be the second Person
in the wonder dance of Three
how could He possibly be housed
inside a womb, upon a tree

the highest heavens are His throne
the earth, the place He rests His feet
what do they think as He comes down
in one small Man, He is complete

—Jodi Cowles

Questions for Discussion

1. Have you ever considered what the angels were thinking about as Jesus prepared to come down to earth? What do you think they might have been thinking?

2. Do you think "waiting" is experienced in the same way in heaven as we experience it on earth? How might it be different?

3. What are you waiting for right now? If you were to look at it from the perspective of a heavenly being, would that change how you wait?

Optional Activity

Google "images from the Hubble telescope" and have each person pick a favorite. Share with one another what looking at the image makes you think about God.

Lighting the Advent Candle

Choose one person (a child if available) to light the first candle. Then ask someone to read the scriptures below.

Isaiah 40:21-26

Do you not know?
Have you not heard?
Has it not been told you from the beginning?
Have you not understood since the earth was founded?
He sits enthroned above the circle of the earth,

and its people are like grasshoppers.
He stretches out the heavens like a canopy,
and spreads them out like a tent to live in.
He brings princes to naught
and reduces the rulers of this world to nothing.
No sooner are they planted,
no sooner are they sown,
no sooner do they take root in the ground,
than he blows on them and they wither,
and a whirlwind sweeps them away like chaff.

"To whom will you compare me?
Or who is my equal?" says the Holy One.
Lift up your eyes and look to the heavens:
Who created all these?
He who brings out the starry host one by one
and calls forth each of them by name.
Because of his great power and mighty strength,
not one of them is missing.

Sing a Song

Sing a song together! Whether you sing beautifully or badly, the point is to sing with abandon and joy in your heart.

Silent Night

Silent night, holy night!
All is calm, all is bright.
Round yon Virgin, Mother and Child.
Holy infant so tender and mild,

Sleep in heavenly peace,
Sleep in heavenly peace.

Silent night, holy night!
Shepherds quake at the sight.
Glories stream from heaven afar
Heavenly hosts sing Alleluia,
Christ the Saviour is born!
Christ the Saviour is born

Silent night, holy night!
Son of God love's pure light.
Radiant beams from Thy holy face
With dawn of redeeming grace,
Jesus Lord, at Thy birth
Jesus Lord, at Thy birth

Close in Prayer

Before your time comes to a close, take a few moments to pray for one another. These don't have to be long or eloquent prayers. But lift one another up by name before God. Ask for any specific prayer requests and allow time for everyone to pray who wants to pray. Ask for one person to close your prayer time.

AND

A small word—and—connects heaven and nature to sing praise to the coming King, but that small connection makes a world of difference.

The connection is evidence of love from a God who wouldn't take no for an answer. He continued the story with a solution to the darkness: Light. The world was bent on darkness and the arrival of Jesus shifted the end of the story.

Hope went from a far-off dream to a livable reality because of God's determination to see His kingdom come on earth and in heaven.

week 2 – monday

Praise the Lord.

Praise the Lord, you his servants;
praise the name of the Lord.

Let the name of the Lord be praised,
both now and forevermore.
From the rising of the sun to the place where it sets,
the name of the Lord is to be praised.

The Lord is exalted over all the nations,
his glory above the heavens.

Who is like the Lord our God,
the One who sits enthroned on high,
who stoops down to look
on the heavens and the earth?

He raises the poor from the dust
and lifts the needy from the ash heap;
he seats them with princes,
with the princes of his people.

He settles the childless woman in her home
as a happy mother of children.

Praise the Lord.
Psalm 113

Small words sometimes have the biggest meaning. Whether represented by three little letters A-N-D or by a swirly, curly symbol "&," the word "and" connects two things together. People are indelibly connected like, "Romeo and Juliet." Two edible ingredients connected together like, "peanut butter and jelly" create a gold standard for school lunch. The physical world connects "day and night" as dissimilar sides of a 24-hour cycle connected into one rhythmic, manageable unit of time. The season of Advent celebrates an unexpected, life-altering connection: heaven and earth. From the first verse in Genesis, *"In the beginning, God created the heavens and the earth,"* to the end of Revelation (21:1), *"I saw a new heaven and a new earth,"* heaven and earth are connected. Heaven and earth have always been connected, but the connection crystalized with Jesus' arrival on earth, making him the "and" between heaven and earth. His departure from a place of perfection, piercing into a world bent on destruction, changed everything for all time and solidified and personified the connection between heaven and earth. Jesus connects heaven to earth, earth to heaven, and the reality of that connection carries enough weight that a long, pondering preparation of heart and mind through the season of Advent is necessary. How can it be that the perfection, holiness, and breadth of heaven connect to the struggle and smudges of the earth?

Before Jesus, during the time of the Old Testament, the world walked in darkness and the few recorded interactions between heaven and earth were miraculous and spectacular. There was an un-singed burning bush, dry land at the bottom of the sea, fire from heaven, and a sea creature who spat out a disobedient man. To attract the attention of humankind and to make a point, God had to be obvious. Heaven and earth connected, and when they did, there were explosions. Then, for many generations, there was no fire, no explosions, no visible connection between heaven and earth.

Until Jesus. He was subtle and unassuming in His delivery, but His new way was world-altering. When Jesus walked as a man on earth, the connection was obvious to most of the people He encountered. The sick were made well, the lame could walk, and the blind could see. He unbridled the world from the restrictive burden of man-made religious law to reveal a new way, different from the way it had always been. But the people with power did their best to squelch the explosive nature of His message by killing Him. And yet, even death couldn't contain Him, and His never-before-seen, one-time resurrection was the match to a smoldering fire, fanned to flame by the new, constant presence of the Holy Spirit.

Without God's unforgettable, large-scale methods of connecting Jesus' physical presence here on earth, where do heaven and earth overlap today? In a world determined to fold in on itself environmentally, politically, and relationally, it seems as though a visible explosion of heaven on earth would be helpful right about now. But the work of drawing attention to where heaven and earth overlap tends to happen explosion-free. Transformation is not flashy, but occurs in the quiet, unseen work of faithful participants.

Though she's never advertised or drawn any attention to herself for it, my mom is a faithful prayer. I haven't seen her methods with my own eyes, but I've heard rumors she has prayer cards and a schedule that faithfully rotates through the cards praying over each person and request each week. The cards gets updated and added to. Requests get scratched off when answered and replaced with something new. She prays for something until she's given an update. Her faithful work is done quietly and continuously. Even if she was on social media, she'd never make a reel humble bragging about her latest prayer time or answered request. She'd never mask some juicy gossip and share it as a "prayer request." She just prays. Heaven overlaps earth in the sincere prayers of my wonderful mom. Her life reflects a light-filled way of life by loving in a way the world is not used to seeing.

Heaven connects to earth through Jesus. He is the "and" who stretched His arms out wide on a cross, connecting God to humanity and humanity to God through His willing sacrifice. As we ponder our own connection to Jesus and how we live out the reality of that connection in the world, may we realign with this perfect "And" and participate in the *good news of great joy for all people.* (paraphrase of Luke 2:10)

— **Rachael Mitchell**

Reflect & Respond

Where do you see the overlap between heaven and earth in your own life today?

If they don't overlap what could change that?

week 2 - tuesday

"I am the Alpha and the Omega," says the Lord God,
*"who is, and who was, and who is to come,
the Almighty."*
Revelation 1:8

The simple three-letter word "*and*" is used by each of us multiple times a day. It is a helpful conjunction that joins words and phrases, indicating a relationship between the connected elements.

Throughout Scripture, we come to know the person of Jesus Christ. His role is defined in part by the hundreds of names and titles given to Him throughout the Bible. Four unique names for Jesus in the biblical text use "*and*" as part of the description. In the names listed below, "*and*" functions as a conjunction, but there is more to notice here. "*And*" is used here to connect two things while also communicating "*in addition to*." Jesus embodies this first name listed but is also *more* than that. He fully embodies the additional names following the conjunction "*and.*"

Jesus is more than we expect. He is the God of abundance who exceeds anything we can ask for or imagine.

Alpha *and* Omega - *"I am the Alpha and the Omega," says the Lord God, "who is, and who was, and who is to come, the Almighty."* (Revelation 1:8) Alpha and Omega are the first and last letters of the Greek alphabet, representing the beginning and the end. This passage in Revelation reveals that Jesus is the beginning and the end while also present with everything in the middle. He was, is, and is to come. Jesus holds all things together and is in all things. Jesus is not only the Alpha, He is also the Omega, and He is everything that was, is, and is yet to come in between.

Author *and* Finisher of our Faith - *Looking unto Jesus the author and finisher of our faith; who for the joy that was set before him endured the cross, despising the shame, and is set down at the right hand of the throne of God.* (Hebrews 12:2) Jesus is the greatest storyteller. His life story is full of mystery, wonder, twists, and turns. It was not at all predictable or expected. The story Jesus is writing on the earth, which encompasses our individual stories, culminates in ways we could not have predicted. The presence of the word *and* in this name for Jesus promises that He will finish what He starts. Every good story has conflict and resolution. A good story is in the making if you find yourself in conflict. The resolution is coming. Jesus is not only the author but also the one who sticks around and finishes the story. With Jesus, we get more than we bargained for.

The Shepherd *and* Overseer of Souls - *For "you were like sheep going astray," but now you have returned to the Shepherd and Overseer of your souls.* (1 Peter 2:25) Jesus leaves the flock to seek after the one. He is the good Shepherd who gently leads us back to the safety and security of His love. As the Overseer of souls, Jesus tends not only to our external needs but also to our internal longings and questions. He is tender and present to our bodies, minds, and souls. We see the abundance of God at work through the person of Jesus.

The Way, the Truth, *and* the Life - *Jesus answered, "I am the way and the truth and the life. No one comes to the Father except through me."* (John 14:6) This name for Jesus is directional, purposeful, and promising. Jesus' life points us to how we are to walk out our faith. He is our trusted guide, lighting the path for us. He is the person of Truth, fulfilling the promises of God through his life, death, and resurrection. He came to give us abundant life and freedom from sin and shame. He offers us joy instead of mourning.

Each name for Jesus reveals His presence in and through time—as we heal, grow, wait, and develop. Jesus is present with us in the "and" of Advent as we wait in tension for what is yet to be realized. I find comfort in knowing that Jesus goes before and behind me while actively engaging with me in the messy middle. Wherever you are in your journey, Jesus is present in the mess *and* purposeful in the details.

— **Connie Armerding**

Reflect & Respond

Entering into the "and" of Advent means embracing tension, angst, and growing pains. What have you found true about God's character in the waiting? What are you learning now that adds more fullness to the story God is writing with your life? I don't know about you, but I don't want the beginning without the end.

Reflect on these names of Jesus:

- Alpha and Omega
- Author and Finisher of our Faith
- The Way, the Truth, and the Life
- The Shepherd and Overseer of Souls

Which name for Jesus is hard for you to connect with? Spend time in prayer now, asking Jesus to reveal to you the part of His character and presence that feels disconnected. He desires to know you and be known by you. Jesus is pursuing your heart, and His love for you is personal.

week 2 - wednesday

*Do nothing from selfish ambition or conceit, but in
humility count others more significant than yourselves. Let each of you look not only to his own
interests, but also to the interests of others.*
Philippians 2:3-4 (ESV)

From my earliest days playing outside my home or camping with
my family in the majestic beauty of Yosemite National Park, I found
great joy in nature. Creation has always spoken to me more clearly
than scripture verses, but there were cautionary voices using words
like "animism" and "worldliness" that kept me silenced until I realized that "heaven" *and* "nature" are indeed woven together. I have
since discovered many spiritual insights simply by observing the
intricate interconnectedness of living organisms, from the smallest
insects to the largest sequoias.

Some of my favorite instructors for the concept of *and* in the forest
are the beautiful creations called lichens. These magical organisms

have everything to do with *and*. They are built by *and*. They exist because of *and*. They thrive because of *and*.

You have most likely encountered lichens many times in your life, sat upon them as you rested on a boulder, scraped them off of your fence, planter boxes, or stepping stones. An unexpected benefit for me during our recent "stay home" orders during the pandemic was time to read books and articles about forest health combined with the opportunity to explore the woods surrounding my home in real time. Reading about nurse logs or the wonders of the underground mycelium network is fine, but actually watching baby seedlings grow taller each year or seeing fungi push their way up through the forest floor is nothing short of magical. This was also when I began appreciating the vast variety of lichens attached to the tree trunks, branches, twigs, and rocks alike.

But what exactly are lichens? They're neither an animal nor a plant, but rather a composite organism made up primarily of an alga and a fungus. Because of the vast number of various algae (*pl*) and fungi (*pl*), the named varieties of lichens are in the thousands in a beautiful array of colors and shapes. Some have the appearance and texture of kale while others look like tiny moose antlers or long stringy hair or balls of steel wool. Observing one tree trunk can reveal dozens of varieties of lichens.

The list of attributes of lichens for forest health is also extensive. They provide nesting materials for birds and rodents as well as a food source for elk and reindeer. They help protect trees from extreme weather conditions, absorbing moisture in damp weather to provide nourishment in dry times. A piece of lichen an inch and a half long can be twenty to thirty years old, so it's important to observe it gently with the reverence it deserves. I used to mistake brittle lichens for dead in the summer months, but I've come to discover that they are still very much alive, even in their crispy state. They are simply waiting for moisture to rehydrate and become pliable once again. Appreciating the many special qualities of lichens has taught me to leave them undisturbed so they can continue to thrive and contribute to their environment.

The beautiful thing about lichens, beyond their unique appearances, is the symbiotic relationship between the alga and the fungus. A symbiotic relationship is one in which organisms exist together in a way that benefits both. Their separate unique abilities are essential for their combined survival. The alga is able to photosynthesize, producing nutrients from sunlight, but it lacks a structure on which to form. Meanwhile, the fungus has a structure but no ability to feed itself. This is where the alga steps in with photosynthesis. I like to think of it as the alga cheerfully preparing breakfast, lunch, and supper to feed the fungus, who is busy building their house. For each, there would be no food or shelter or survival without each other. Instead, they have formed a beautiful new organism called lichen. Alga + fungus = lichen. Symbiosis. Working together for their common good.

Jesus was sent to earth to call us to love and serve one another in a symbiotic fashion. Every act of compassion here on earth for those on the margins is reminiscent of the alga and fungus providing for each other. So too are the moments of loving one's neighbor, or creating artistic, literary, or musical beauty that calls people to rise above the petty fears of the day. Jesus' call has been carried out over the centuries in the efforts of care providers during plagues and in the heroic actions of disaster rescuers. It continues today in those speaking out against injustice, in sharing a meal, changing a diaper, picking up litter, caring for a loved one, caring for a stranger. These selfless acts bless the provider as well as the recipient.

Nature is clearly one of heaven's teachers of the eternal principles of interdependence and mutual appreciation. Just as the symbiotic lichens have the unique ability to remove selected air pollutants from the atmosphere, we are able to have a similar purifying effect, driving out isolation, loneliness, despair, fear. May we all find ways to work together for the goodness of all.

— **Donna Dahlstrom**

Reflect & Respond

With whom have you experienced a "symbiotic" relationship as you each contributed to the well-being of the other?

Consider sending them a note this week to say, "Thank you for being in my life."

week 2 – thursday

You have turned my mourning into dancing; you have
loosed my sackcloth and clothed me with gladness.
Psalm 30:11

"Everything feels different this year," my son says as he hangs the first ornament on the tree. A white porcelain snowflake with delicate gold lettering marking the year nestles against the faux evergreen. Honestly, its beauty doesn't match the oddity of the season or the year we've survived.

Since we took down the tree eleven months ago, we've added a puppy to our family mix, moved into a new home, nursed our son through a concussion, oh… and we've been living through a global pandemic. Our move was anything but smooth, but people close to us lost loved ones. All of us have lost our sense of security. Life is out of rhythm.

I pop open each of the storage bins holding Christmas decorations, then step back and sink into our gray rocking recliner to survey the tree and living room, to contemplate and to make plans; I take a sip of coffee. *College Gameday* plays on the TV. I hold a red mug in my hands, noting the message "cup of cheer" inscribed across the mug. I wish cheer came as easily as sipping the sweet, creamy coffee.

In our home, we decorate for Christmas around Thanksgiving. Usually, I stay in my pajamas (carefully chosen festive ones!) and drink at least two cups of coffee, followed by hot tea or something else from a mug. My husband and son are in charge of lugging the tree down from storage and setting it up in the designated location. I usually pull out each item I think I'll use and set them on or around the kitchen counter so I can remember what holiday decorations I have available. Then I get to work, adding a feeling of festivity to our home.

When I'm satisfied with the trimmings, or the day is done, I pack up anything I haven't used and stow it back in the bins. I have a system that has worked for the last eight years, but this year—in a new home, in a different head and heart space—adorning our home for the holidays feels different, heavier, and unsettled.

With resolution, I stand to finish the Christmas decorations. I promise myself I'll keep it simple this year. One by one, I pull the ornaments from bins and carefully place them on the tree. Each ornament tells a story, and I take time to remember as I place them on the tree—an ornament for each year since our family was established, a bauble from each past family vacation, and a few vintage beauties from my childhood. Next, I drape the mantle in red shimmery tulle, arrange the figurines of the Nativity scene, and nestle a strand of warm, white lights around the display. Mary, Joseph, and Jesus sit in the middle, with shepherds and barn animals around. I set the wise men off to the side in my quiet attempt at Biblical accuracy since they weren't actually in Bethlehem for the birth. I hang mistletoe, then display our stockings—one extra for our two dogs, since they share, make four—and replace a few pictures on the wall with holiday reminders to "believe." My favorite picture, one of Santa kneeling beside a Nativity scene, takes center stage in our home's entryway.

Finally, that evening, I snap the lids back on the empty bins and lug them all back upstairs. Evening has fallen. Back downstairs, I place the lid on the pumpkin pie candle, which has been lit each evening in the fall, and move it into the cabinet. I slide a new one out and pop the lid open. With a quick light, the smell of cinnamon soon fills the room.

As the day ends, I settle into the couch and cover myself with a knitted red blanket. Before I turn my attention to the football game on television, I again survey the living room, now festive and celebratory. My heavy heart becomes a little lighter, anticipating the celebration of the One who turns our wailing into dancing. I exhale into a feeling of gratefulness.

In Psalm 30 we read David's praises to the Lord following a difficult, perhaps near-death, experience. He celebrates the Lord's help and favor, claiming the rejoicing that comes in the morning. The Lord heard his cries and turned wailing into dancing. There is difficulty in this season, but rejoicing can return.

So, as the difficult year comes to a close, our family chooses to celebrate–with decorations and even some dancing.

I relish the festive reds and evergreens and twinkling lights in our home and am thankful for the three of us being home together each evening. And I wish our extended family was closer to enjoy these evenings with us.

In this year I promise myself I'll make merry with a few, and I acknowledge I'll grieve large gatherings canceled by a virus.

I can savor the quiet, and long for the gregariously social. I'm learning depth of life is found in the "and."

— **Bethany McMillon**

Reflect & Respond

As we celebrate the season, are there feelings that seem to conflict?

Can we acknowledge both joy and mourning?

week 2 - friday

*The Holy Spirit will come on you, and the power of
the Most High will overshadow you. So the holy one
to be born will be called the Son of God.*
Luke 1:35

The concept of the Holy Trinity is a difficult one for Christians and seekers of faith alike. How can Jesus be God and God be Jesus and both of them also be the Holy Spirit, three-in-one? The best way the Holy Trinity has been explained to me, during the first years of my Christian walk, was that God the Father is the creator and sustainer of all things. God the Son is God in the flesh, as a human being, on Earth. And God the Holy Spirit—the power of God which is active in the world—is the mighty counselor, helper, and confidante that Jesus left with believers when He said goodbye to His disciples for the last time.

As a child, the concept of the Holy Spirit frightened me. When He was referenced in our small Presbyterian church, it was as the "Godhead," the trio of the Holy Spirit being God along with the

Father and the Son. This was perplexing to my middle school-aged brain. On the rare occasion we visited the Catholic church of my mother's youth, I understood Him to be "the Holy Ghost." What was this Ghost and this Godhead? I don't know about you, but I didn't want a ghost near me, no matter how holy–much less inside my heart. I believe I thought He might be the dead spirit of Jesus who would haunt me to ensure I was behaving at all times. It's a confusing concept to many, yet New Testament scriptures reference the Holy Spirit at least 90 times. The Holy Spirit is important to those of us who are followers of Jesus, as we understand Him to be God with us, at all times.

One thing to note is that the Spirit is rarely referenced without the Father *and* the Son. The word "and" can be defined as "used to join two words that are the same, making their meaning stronger." I think this is a fitting definition because the Father, along with the Son and the Spirit, makes the trio stronger indeed. You won't find the story of the Trinity without the word "and" to join the three forces together for the good of all mankind. You won't find the word "and" in any description of Jesus that isn't describing His beautifully loving and grace-filled heart.

During this Christmas season, when families are eager to partake in the traditions of presents, trees, carols, hot chocolate, and cozy family gatherings, fraught with overindulgence, let's take a moment to dig into the "ands" of the Trinity—the God who loves us so much that He created the world to dwell with us in it, the Spirit who has been here since the beginning of that creation, and Jesus— His birth and short life among us, His death on the cross, and His eternal love for us, seen through the teachings of His disciples after His resurrection.

When God created the heavens and the earth, the Holy Spirit was there when, "*the earth was formless and empty, darkness was over the surface of the deep, **and** the Spirit of God was hovering over the waters.*" (Genesis 1:2)

When Mary, the virgin bride-to-be, was visited by the angel Gabriel, she was told, "*The Holy Spirit will come on you, **and** the power of the Most High will overshadow you. So the holy one to be born will be called the Son of God.*" (Luke 1:35)

When Jesus was born, after His parents made the arduous trek to Bethlehem to be counted, scripture tells us, "*Unto us a child is born, to us a son is given, and the government will be on his shoulders. **And** he will be called Wonderful Counselor, Mighty God, Everlasting Father, Prince of Peace.*" (Isaiah 9:6)

When Jesus was baptized at the start of His public ministry, "*He went up out of the water. At that moment heaven was opened, **and** he saw the Spirit of God descending like a dove **and** alighting on him.*" (Matthew 16:17)

When Jesus knew His time had come to leave His disciples and suffer for the sins of the world, He said, "***And** I will ask the Father, **and** he will give you another advocate to help you **and** be with you forever—the Spirit of truth. The world cannot accept him, because it neither sees him nor knows him. But you know him, for he lives with you **and** will be in you.*" (John 14:16-17)

When Jesus was resurrected and his disciples traveled the world to share the good news, John, in exile on the island of Patmos, wrote, "*For there are three that testify: the Spirit, the water, and the blood; **and** the three are in agreement.*" (1 John 5 7-8)

The apostle Paul, concerned as he sought to preserve the unity of the body of believers in Corinth, said, *"Now it is God who makes both us and you stand firm in Christ. He anointed us, set his seal of ownership on us, **and** put his Spirit in our hearts as a deposit, guaranteeing what is to come."* (2 Corinthians 1:21-22)

Friends, when you celebrate Christ this December (and every day), and as you experience the giddiness and joy of selecting the perfect gifts, take a moment to reflect on the gifts Jesus gave *you*—His earthly birth, marking hope and healing to a broken world, and the Spirit given upon His death and resurrection to be a conduit between us and the heavenly realms!

— **Indee Musa**

Reflect & Respond

How can the relationship and interdependence among the Father, Son, and Holy Spirit inspire your family to cultivate stronger bonds and healthy connections? Think about and discuss how the Trinity can serve as a guide for promoting a spirit of togetherness and unity in each of you.

AND

week 2 – saturday

On the seventh day God had finished his work of creation, so he rested from all his work. And God blessed the seventh day and declared it holy, because it was the day when he rested from all his work of creation.
Genesis 2:2–3 (NLT)

December. The time of year when there seems to be a never-ending list of activities and events and chores and shopping and decorating and parties and holiday movies and baking and gift exchanges and out-of-town guests and twinkling lights and cards and gingerbread houses and carols and…and…and….

This was my approach to December for a long time. I crammed our family calendar full of festive activities, to-do lists, and events because I thought these were the things that made the season complete. The genius of the Christmas "and" meant I could simply add more and more and more to our holiday plate until it was overflowing like a stocking on Christmas morning. I thought the "and" was what made for a magical Christmas. But no matter how many "and's" I added, come Christmas morning, I would inevitably find myself worn out, worthless, and wanting nothing more than to crawl back into bed and hibernate until the New Year.

We often approach December believing that a calendar full of cheerful events will make us feel holly and jolly all month long. While the gift of "and" at Christmas does allow for more things to be added to our holiday season, I wonder if it's time to consider a different approach to the "and" of Christmas.

When I look back at the creation story in Genesis, I see that our all-powerful Creator God didn't use "and" to add more to the masterpiece He'd created; rather, He used "and" to rest. *"And God blessed the seventh day and declared it holy, because it was the day when he rested from all his work of creation."* (Gen. 2:3) God did more in the first six days of creation than I ever could consider accomplishing in 25 days of December, and yet He recognized the importance of taking time to rest. Why did God think rest was the best thing to round out our seven-day week?

I think it's because He knows that rest happens in the "and" moments of our life. We are human beings, not the Creator of the Universe. In spite of the advancements in health and technology, we do have a limited supply of energy. We can't just keep going and going and going like the Energizer Bunny. There comes a point when our bodies need to power down to sleep, our minds need to be understimulated, and our spirits need more than a brief moment of peace. Rest is required for our bodies and minds to function properly. But rest is also required for our spirits to heal. Rest is physical, mental, and spiritual. God, who has existed since the beginning, who has no end, and who is the most powerful being in the entire universe, rested. So why don't we?

I think it's because we are afraid to rest. If we slow down long enough to let our spirits catch up with the pace of our lives, it might shock us to see what we find. Disappointment? Resentment? Unforgiveness? Apathy? Greed? Pride? Slowing down to rest means we might have to become aware of the things we've been working very hard to ignore.

Rest requires us to be still, to be quiet, to reflect, and to consider that maybe the pace of the life we're living isn't all that healthy or helpful after all. Sure, our hustle may impress others and we might be accumulating a lot of stuff along the way, but at what cost?

I can't think of a better time than Christmas to start being more intentional about resting. Jesus didn't come so we could do life and carry all of its responsibilities ourselves. In fact, it was Jesus who said, *"Come to me, all of you who are weary and carry heavy burdens, and I will give you rest."* (Matthew 11:28)

Jesus is the best "and" we could add to our lives this Christmas. Inviting Him into our lives means we invite His spirit of peace to rule in our hearts. He trades our worn-out, weary hearts for an eternity of resting in his arms. How will you answer His invitation to come and rest this holiday season?

— **Leslee Stewart**

Refleci & Respond

What place does rest have in your life?

What are some of the "and's" you tend to add to your plate in December?

What can you do over the next month to replace these with intentional moments of rest?

How will you hold yourself accountable for making rest a priority?

The second Sunday of Advent

On Sundays during Advent, we encourage you to gather with family and friends to enjoy fellowship and a time of encountering God together during the holiday season. (The devotion can also be done individually.)

During your time, you will be reading a reflection poem, discussing a few questions, participating in an optional exercise, and ending the time by lighting the second Advent candle, singing a song, and reading scripture. Make sure everything is ready before you begin.

Ask someone to read the Reflection out loud:

> *we're walking in the and*
> *and in the not yet, not quite yet*
> *we're living in the in-between*
> *with our great hope still unmet*
>
> *You've paid our ugly debt*
> *and for that there is no defining*
> *the joy we feel, the shame that's gone*
> *the peace and the refining*

we're walking in our robes of white
and trying not to sully
but every day the mud and dust
arises in the gully

we sit here in the certainty
of hope that's not yet seen
and vibrate in the discontent
the squeeze of in between

the and of all this bloody earth
the and of evil and of joy
the and of deep forgiveness
yet we fall for every ploy

the and of being Yours
and having all our sins wiped clean
but bitter prowls the enemy
down here in the in-between

we live here in the and
of deep, abiding certainty
of what is sealed for us in heaven
and of the day when we'll go free

the and of bitter trials
and the grim certainty of grief
greatly rejoicing in the midst
we wait in hope for our relief

the and of an inheritance
that will never spoil or perish
yet surrounded by the suffering
and the death of those we cherish

You chose us for this and
just as You chose us for Your home
and so we ask for strength today
to just be Yours and Yours alone

we wait here in the and
we're waiting for Your kingdom come
we wait for evil things, at last
to finally, truly come undone

we wait for tears and deep regret
to fade as we behold Your wonder
and we join the mighty chorus
as You rip the and *asunder*

— **Jodi Cowles**

Questions for Discussion

1. Is there an "and" that is particularly difficult for you in this season?

2. What are you most looking forward to when the time of "and" has passed?

3. How would you describe the living hope we've been born into? Have you experienced it?

Optional Activity

Take a few minutes and have everyone draw a picture or write a few words about/expressing what comes to your mind about the word "and." Share your thoughts with one another, whether you're a Picasso or not!

Lighting the Advent Candle

Choose one person (a child if available) to light the second candle. Then ask someone to read the scriptures below.

1 Peter 1:3-9:

Praise be to the God and Father of our Lord Jesus Christ! In his great mercy he has given us new birth into a living hope through the resurrection of Jesus Christ from the dead, and into an inheritance that can never perish, spoil or fade. This inheritance is kept in heaven for you, who through faith are shielded by God's power until the coming of the salvation that is ready to be revealed in the last time. In all this you greatly rejoice, though now for a little while you may have had to suffer grief in all kinds of trials. These have come so that the proven genuineness of your faith—of greater worth than gold, which perishes even though refined by fire—may result in praise, glory and honor when Jesus Christ is revealed. Though you have not seen him, you love him; and even though you do not see him now, you believe in him and are filled with an inexpressible and glorious joy, for you are receiving the end result of your faith, the salvation of your souls.

Sing a Song

Sing a song together! Whether you sing beautifully or badly, the point is to sing with abandon and joy in your heart.

O Come All Ye Faithful

O come, all ye faithful,
Joyful and triumphant!
O come ye, O come ye to Bethlehem!
Come and behold Him,
Born the King of angels;
O come, let us adore Him,
O come, let us adore Him,
O come, let us adore Him,
Christ, the Lord!

Sing, choirs of angels,
Sing in exaltation,

Sing, all ye citizens of heav'n above;
Glory to God,
All glory in the highest!
O come, let us adore Him,
O come, let us adore Him,
O come, let us adore Him,
Christ, the Lord!

For He alone is worthy,
For He alone is worthy,
For He alone is worthy,
Christ, the Lord.

Close in Prayer

Before your time comes to a close, take a few moments to pray for one another. These don't have to be long or eloquent prayers. But lift one another up by name before God. Ask for any specific prayer requests and allow time for everyone to pray who wants to pray. Ask for one person to close your prayer time.

NATURE

Whether it's observed on a micro or macro level, nature is a constant symphony of praise back to its Creator.

The systems, design, and colors reflect the order, intellect, and creativity of a God who created not just a functional environment for life, but a place of beauty to reside.

And we ourselves reflect His nature. A bit of who He is shows up in a little bit of who we are and that good news cultivates hope and light here on earth.

NATURE

week 3 – monday

*God created everything through him, and nothing
was created except through him. The Word gave life
to everything that was created, and his life
brought light to everyone.*
John 1:3-4 (NLT)

One thing I love to do is travel, especially to places with incredible natural beauty like the Rocky Mountains or the Pacific Northwest. Seeing the majesty of waterfalls tumbling down a granite cliff face or towering pine trees that seem to reach all the way to the floor of heaven never ceases to amaze me.

No matter where my travels take me—from the ocean to the desert, to rolling country hills—one thing about the various landscapes I've experienced remains true: *Nature doesn't need any enhancements to be appreciated.* Flowers don't need a fancy camera filter to make their colors pop. Birds don't need Auto-Tune to make their songs ring true. And snow-covered mountains don't need AI-generated imaging to take our breath away. They are all beautiful the way God created them.

In the opening verses of John 1, we see that Jesus (whom John calls "the Word") was with God before creation began, and it was through Jesus that God created everything that was made:

- Day and night (Genesis 1:2-5)

- The sky (Genesis 1:6-8)

- Land, seas, trees, and vegetation (Genesis 1:9-13)

- The sun, moon, and stars (Genesis 1:14-19)

- Animals, fish, and birds (Genesis 1:20-25)

- Man and woman (Genesis 1:26-31, 2:18-25)

John 1:4 says Jesus gave life to everything that was created. God didn't need anything extra in order to create the majesty of the world; creation was made perfect and brought to life through Jesus.

So, if God made creation perfect in its natural state, why don't we see ourselves the same way?

Too often we devalue ourselves, seeing our flaws and failures as a barrier to being accepted. We think we need a different number on the scale or a certain amount in our bank account to feel valued. The right neighborhood means we've made it and a job title can affirm our worth. When we settle for anything less, society says we must be lacking in some way.

We often approach our relationship with God the same way, thinking we have to be cleaned up, have it all together, and be perfect before we can know Him. If we came to Him in our natural state with our anxiety, fear, anger, doubt, greed, or disappointment showing, there is no way He would want anything to do with us. *Right?*

Wrong. God, through Jesus, created us in His image (Genesis 1:27) and He called us very good (Genesis 1:31). Yet He also knew it would be impossible for us to live perfectly, to be sinless, so He sent His only Son, Jesus, the only one who knew no sin, to be the sacrifice for ours and reconcile us back to God (2 Corinthians 5:19-21).

The night Christ was born, there was no filter making the manger look more appealing to Mary and Joseph. And I'm sure the shepherds didn't smell fantastic when they arrived to see for themselves what the angels had been singing about. Everything about that first Christmas was raw, real, and natural, including the arrival of Jesus as a naked, tiny, human baby.

Yet all who witnessed that first Christmas night saw beauty when they beheld the Messiah, the Son of God, the light of the world. They couldn't stop singing praises and glorifying God for what they had heard and seen. They knew that baby was absolutely perfect in His natural state.

And so are you.

Jesus is inviting you to come to Him just as you are, in your natural state. You don't need any enhancements or filters to be His friend. No polish or shine is required to be in His presence. You don't have to have the perfect words to talk to Him. He created you, He sees you, He knows you, and He loves you just the way you are. Let that truth sink deep into your spirit as you invite Him to be the light in your life this Christmas.

— Leslee Stewart

Reflect & Respond

What is one of the most beautiful places you've ever seen? Why is it so beautiful to you?

Thinking of the first Christmas, what do you think were some of the natural sights, sounds, smells, and experiences that the "TV version" of that story often leaves out?

Do you ever struggle to feel worthy of God's love? If so, why?

Name one thing you like or appreciate about yourself (it could be something physical, mental, emotional, or spiritual).

What is one thing you can do this Christmas to remind yourself that you are loved by God, just as you are?

week 3 - tuesday

Let the fields be jubilant, and everything in them;
let all the trees of the forest sing for joy.
Psalm 96:12

Forests are glorious. God's handiwork, perfectly spoken into existence, is on display everywhere in a forest. People have always been in awe of forests and the nature they contain, but many forest lovers are unaware of the exponentially more complex creation beneath the trees. God created intricate systems for trees to communicate and support other trees. This example in nature reminds me of how His children are to support and rely on each other.

Under the forest floor lie the complex, fascinating *mycorrhizal* (fungal root) networks that trees use to send specific nutrients and electrical and distress signals to each other. As scientists research these connections, they have discovered that in healthy forest ecosystems, these fungal networks connect back to mother trees. The mother tree is almost always the oldest tree with the highest number of and farthest-reaching mycorrhizal connections in the forest.

Trees can determine if a nearby tree of their kind is lacking a certain amount of carbon dioxide or send an electrical warning signal that a specific type of beetle is infiltrating their bark. Recent discoveries show how the mycorrhizal network of a mother tree reaches farther and more intimately than any other tree in a forest. It can coordinate an entire forest.

The most important groups mother trees support are saplings and young trees. Saplings are highly susceptible to extreme environmental factors as well as being the most disadvantaged in the recovery process, but they survive using mycorrhizal networks. Extreme environmental conditions are some of the most common and devastating events trees can experience. Every sapling that breaks the surface of the earth is a miracle; often, it is quite literally one in a million seeds a tree releases. There are endless factors that prevent seeds from reaching germination after being released from a tree. Sometimes, a seed must wait multiple years before determining if the environment is safe enough to sprout. While it germinates, it is at its most vulnerable to its lifetime enemies: hungry fungi, animals, and insects. Hundreds of thousands of seeds fail to sprout making a small green shoot breaking through the soil a triumphant miracle.

As a sapling grows, it becomes vulnerable to extreme environmental factors; it has almost no control over what happens to it. Scientists have begun to classify the factors that threaten the vulnerable saplings, or "trauma." Young trees and saplings are shaped by their "childhood" environments. For example, trees that not only experienced but survived drought in their early years have been observed to absorb and store every drop of water in a rainstorm. In an arid environment, this is a helpful skill, but in an environment where the drought was an exception, these trees will struggle for the rest of their lives. However, God's design of healthy forest ecosystems, supported by mother trees, allows young trees to recover from trauma. In their youth, afflicted saplings can use mycorrhizal systems to send electrical distress signals throughout the forest to the mother tree. Mother trees are essential in assessing the signal and sending nutrients back through the fungal networks to the distressed sapling. When the forest assists saplings, dangerous trauma responses in trees can be avoided. God's perfect design of the world is clearly shown through mother trees' ability to nurture forests.

Just as mother trees support the vulnerable and weak saplings to build a healthy and sustainable forest, God has designed the Christian community to do the same. We are supposed to encourage our brothers and sisters, support the vulnerable in our communities, and serve the people around us with kindness and generosity. Like trees, humans are also influenced by our environment. From birth, a baby is dependent upon its mother. As they grow, childhood trauma inhibits proper development. The environments of both humans and trees shape what they believe about the world and how they treat others, and many mental afflictions can be traced back to environmental trauma. Many cannot be fully healed and will carry and be inhibited by those responses for the rest of their lives.

But because Jesus came to this natural world, humans have hope. Jesus brings hope for healing, for eternity, and for peace. He provides the "nutrients" people need to recover from traumatic experiences and environments. When we support each other, transformed by Jesus, we can become healthier humans and, in turn, grow stronger communities. We are reminded of God's intent for people to nurture each other through His beautiful design of mother trees to nurture forests.

From delicate but unstoppable mycorrhizal networks to recovering from trauma through healthy ecosystems, God's work is clearly reflected in His creation of mother trees. This intricate system serves as a reminder of the life-changing, community-healing reality of Jesus' presence in our lives. As mother trees nurture forests, so can we nurture each other by following Jesus' example. We cannot help but rejoice in the glory of the community within a forest.

— **Hollis Mitchell**

Reflect & Respond

Which tree do you more strongly identify with: the mother tree or the sapling? Why?

What can you do today to build up the community you're already involved with?

NATURE

week 3 - wednesday

The heavens declare the glory of God;
the skies proclaim the work of his hands.
Day after day they pour forth speech;
night after night they reveal knowledge.
They have no speech, they use no words;
no sound is heard from them.
Yet their voice goes out into all the earth,
their words to the ends of the world.
Psalm 19:1-4

When we feel the weight of the world closing in on us, we need a reminder that we have not been tasked with carrying all of it on our shoulders. It is not up to us. When we step outside our homes, offices, cars, or whatever four walls threaten to close in around us, and breathe in the fresh air of the out-of-doors, our lungs exhale, and so do our souls. When we look up, we find ourselves under a great big sky that encompasses the whole earth. It spans from New York City to Beijing to Sydney … and everything in between. The bigness of the sky reminds us that we are part of a much larger story.

The drive in our culture to do more at a faster pace makes slowing down difficult. But the slowing down is an invitation to notice and to listen. Being in God's creation helps us to order our scattered thoughts and engage all of our senses.

Romans 1:20 tells us that all people can hear God speaking in one way or another: *"For since the creation of the world God's invisible qualities—his eternal power and divine nature—have been clearly seen, being understood from what has been made, so that people are without excuse."*

Are we listening?

When was the last time you saw fresh dew on the morning leaves, clocked a hummingbird flapping its wings 6,000 times a second hovering in place to drink the sweet water from the feeder, or watched the sun tucking in for the evening in the covers of the ocean?

These mundane yet holy moments declare the glory of God. Day after day, we are invited to encounter God through His creation. God's speech is being poured out through nature (Psalm 19:2). There is a consistent flow of the story of the Creator being told through creation.

The Advent story reveals what can happen when God's people receive the message declared through creation. The wise men followed the star because they, *"...saw his star when it rose and... c[ame] to worship him."* (Matthew 2:2) The Bethlehem star was an invitation through nature to learn more about the Creator. The wise men were attentive and attuned, causing them to notice this signpost in the middle of the sky. When we read the ancient text of the Bible, it can be easy to distance ourselves from the story. But the same Creator is still communicating through His creation. God is using His created world to point to the person of Jesus—He was doing it then, and He is doing it now.

It is undeniable that nature calls us into wonder and worship. Remembering how small we are brings perspective, reminding us that we are not in control. When life feels too heavy and too much, let's get outside and let nature nurture us. Relishing the feeling of being small reorients our focus on the bigness of creation and points us to worship the Creator of it all.

He made all things, big and small.

— **Connie Armerding**

Reflect & Respond

What do you notice about God's created world when you slow down enough to see it? What is it that God wants us to see? The star caught the wise men's attention. What would it take to capture your attention?

Take time this week to be still and silent in nature for 20 minutes or longer. Let your eyes wander and your ears open to see and hear what God is saying through creation.

Read Matthew 7:7 and heed its instruction. *Ask. Seek. Knock.* God is speaking and has something specific to say to you.

Write down what you hear God saying, and with gratitude in your heart, thank Him for how He has created nature to nurture our souls. He knew exactly what our chaotic inner world would need to return to a place of peace and rest. He planned it that way.

NATURE

week 3 – thursday

A new command I give you: Love one another.
As I have loved you, so you must love one another.
By this everyone will know that you are my disciples,
if you love one another.
John 13:34-35

One of my all-time favorite Christmas movies is *Elf*. While I also love the classics like *It's a Wonderful Life* and *White Christmas,* there is just something special about the innocence and naiveté of Will Ferrell's character, Buddy the Elf. Buddy loves everyone and everything. He is overjoyed at the simplest of pleasures like pools of maple syrup poured haphazardly over spaghetti or the sound of anyone singing. Buddy's mantra is, "The best way to spread Christmas cheer is singing loud for all to hear." While walking down a New York City street for the very first time, Buddy spots a coffee shop and rushes through the doors excitedly shouting, "Congratulations!" to anyone within earshot. Turns out the sign on the front window reads, "World's best cup of coffee," and Buddy takes that quite literally. Simply put, Buddy sees the best in everyone. It's just his nature.

There is someone infinitely more special, loving, and joy-filled than Buddy, and the kicker is, he's fully human, fully real, and completely present. Of course, that someone is Jesus, and the nature of Jesus is something even more incredible to behold.

Whether or not you believe that Jesus was God in flesh and possessed the nature and characteristics of our God in heaven, you cannot refute the historical evidence that He was, at the very least, a real person who existed in history, and whose impact on humanity was so powerful, it has held up to this very day. While many despised Him, refused to recognize Him, and called for His death, those who follow Him do so for the very nature of who he was (and is!), both divine and human. Jesus's nature was selfless, loving, gentle, joyful, empathetic, neighborly, and sacrificial.

In Jesus' short time on this earth and during His even shorter ministry, He modeled the nature of selflessness when He washed the feet of his disciples and asked that we care for our brothers and sisters in the same way. The people of that time walked around in open sandals in a terrain filled with dirt and sand. You can imagine how dirty one's feet might be! To lay down all stigma or pride, as God incarnate, and to hold and wash the dirty feet of his disciples shows that Jesus valued others before himself.

Jesus experienced deep emotions as well. He became angry when the temple was not used as intended: as a place of prayer for "all nations" (including the Gentiles), but rather for cheating the poor and the widows. This was a righteous anger, aimed at hypocrisy, and not the selfish anger which we humans can readily possess. Jesus felt pain with us. He wept bitterly when his dear friend Lazarus was found to be dead. Jesus knew Lazarus would die before He got to him, and He knew the plan He had to call Lazarus out of his tomb, yet He wept with Mary and Martha. Jesus was feeling the emotional wounds of those He loved dearly, and it grieved Him. He is compassionate in every way.

Jesus' nature is forgiving. As He hung on the cross dying and being mocked by Roman soldiers, His words were still for the good of humanity, *"Father, forgive them, for they know not what they do."* (Luke 23:34) Can you think of a time someone has really hurt you? How easy was it to dole out forgiveness in that moment? Jesus forgave and asks that we do the same.

Jesus' nature was humble. He was superior to mankind in every way, sinless and perfect, yet never seeking accolades or rewards for Himself. Like Jesus, we are to *do nothing from selfish ambition or conceit, but in humility count others more significant than [our]selves."* (Philippians 2:3)

Jesus was gentle. He had empathy for those who suffered and who were broken. He was gentle with the Samaritan woman at the well, seeking her out even though the Jews had a longstanding disdain for the Samaritans. Sharing what He knew to be true of her life, He gently and lovingly offered her water from the living well, changing her heart and future outlook. He was gentle with children, and they loved to come to Him. He healed them, raised them from the dead, and used them as an example of the childlike faith we are to have—pure and accepting.

Most of all, Jesus' nature embodied the purest form of love. Jesus healed the sick in love. He raised the dead in love. He fed the hungry and the poor in love. He ate with the sinners in love, and in the most magnanimous feat of love, He gave His life for us. Jesus asks us to love one another with abandon, to even show love to our enemies, and to love our neighbors as ourselves, not just during the holidays, but every day we are gifted to have here on earth.

— **Indee Musa**

Reflect & Respond

As followers of Christ, we believe the nature of God is one of unconditional and enduring love for all of us. In Greek, this is known as *agape*—the highest form of love. God showed this love by sacrificing His son, Jesus, who possessed a nature of forgiveness, compassion, and service.

Discuss how, in your family, you might each take on some of the nature of Christ by serving and sacrificing for others in your family. What does that look like? Washing Mom's plate after she's cooked your favorite meal? Reading the kiddos a bedtime story when the day has already been so long? Talk about ways you might show this *agape*-type love to other members of your family, this Christmas and every day.

NATURE

week 3 - friday

The steadfast love of the LORD never ceases; his
mercies never come to an end; they are new every
morning; great is your faithfulness.
Lamentations 3:22-23 (ESV)

I have the privilege of living in the midst of a beautiful evergreen forest, lush with Western Hemlock and Silver Fir trees. Each year I marvel over the new little trees that grow taller after being ensconced in snow and ice for the winter. Some have been bent over for many months, and after the spring thaw, they begin to straighten up reaching for the warmth of the sunlight.

There are several trees with wide trunks, indicating their longevity in this location, but there is clear evidence that something dramatic happened in this forest many decades ago. There are numerous stumps, some six feet in diameter, dotted between the thinner trees. History tells us this area was logged to help create a railway through the mountain pass, using the lumber for trestles and railroad ties as well as homes for growing communities farther away.

After the railroad company harvested what it needed, they left the land and divided it into parcels. Over the years, the parcels were sold to families who are now our kind neighbors on this one-mile-long street that is once again surrounded by forest. But how did this happen, this spontaneous reforestation? There were no work crews sent in with buckets of seedlings to plant back in those days. No excellent regulations to plant x number of trees for every one removed. They just took what they needed and moved on. But nature remained. Nature is steadfast. Nature was still at work. Nature found a way.

All of this new growth happened without the intervention (or interference) of humans. Nature found a way. Nature wins every time. The trees became rooted and grounded in the soil of their ancestors. Their roots became intertwined for stability as well as communication through the fibers of the mycelium network. Their branches above became tangled, which led to even greater stability as they sway together in the wind as a unit. The connected canopy above now helps filter the pounding rain before it reaches the delicate seedlings and porous forest floor below. Nature did this on her own. Nature is steadfast.

Fortunately for us, and for the many birds and critters who make their home here, the forest has returned. The abundant flora and fauna now found on Mount St. Helens after her 1980 eruption is another example of the steadfastness of nature, as is the return of the forest in the city of Chernobyl, many years after a nuclear accident. Trees just keep doing what they were designed to do, drawing in nutrients from the soil, and making sugar from the sun. Breathing in carbon dioxide, giving off oxygen. Adding a light-colored ring underneath the bark layer during the warm summer months next to a corresponding dark ring in winter. Year after year after year.

I am not a person who enjoys change. I like predictability. I like routine. But I've lived long enough now to realize that life is always changing. Just around the time I thought I understood my children's needs, they were already in a new phase that I needed to figure out. I planned to be a stay-at-home mom forever and a room parent for every classroom, but financial choices directed me elsewhere. I thought we'd raise our children in the forest, but we were drawn to the city. I assumed we'd retire in the city, but instead, we returned to the forest. Change. Always change.

Throughout these changes, whether they concern my health or the health of a loved one, personal vocation, international conflict, or the economy, I find great comfort in recognizing the steadfastness of nature. This constancy is a reminder that the God of the universe also never changes, pouring out continuous love, provision, and blessing on this world as gifts of unmerited mercy. Every cup of cold water, every bite of food, every moment of life happens because the God who sustains the world of nature never changes.

The 700-year-old hemlock in my neighborhood has been growing since before Europeans set sail or wagons traveled west across the continent, and long before trains needed lumber or families built homes. The hemlock just kept taking in nutrients from the ground below and sunlight from the sky above, growing ring by ring. In a world that is constantly changing, God, as the source of all nature, remains faithful.

— **Donna Dahlstrom**

Reflect & Respond

What reminds you of God's faithful love for you?

NATURE

week 3 – saturday

"... I have come that they may have life and have it to the full."
John 10:10

I step out the door for a mid-morning walk through the neighborhood. The air is brisk, but the sun shines brightly.

In the last few days, the semester has ended, with classroom Christmas parties and holiday festivities with our church groups, shopping and decorating, baking and laughter. After school yesterday, I closed my car door and sat in blissful silence for several minutes, seeking peace and hope for rest in the coming break from school.

The festivities follow on the heels of a semester full of high school learning for my son, a nonstop busy season for my husband, and renovations of my workspace that left my co-workers and me displaced. The day-to-day difficulties wore our energy and spirits thin.

In the first few paces of my walk, down the steps and across the street, I focus my mind on prayer and on releasing the tension I can feel all through my shoulders. A breath in. A breath out. The glorious first morning of Christmas break.

This morning, the continued quiet—a few minutes navigating a nature trail in our neighborhood—restores my heart. I stretch my arms behind my back and then reach high toward the bright blue, cloudless sky as I step. The rhythm of my shoes hitting the pavement path behind our neighborhood, the occasional notes of birdsong or muted voices in the backyards are all that break the silence. My soul begins to find peace even with these intermittent interruptions.

For several moments the solitude continues—just me, bare brown branches stretching toward the sky, golden sun rays peering through, and fat little squirrels that sprint every so often across the pavement. As I round the first bend in the trail, I slow. Brilliant red berries catch my eye. Along the path, their stark crimson, scattered and nestled against the dull brown foliage, shouts the potential and hope of life abundant. Now that I've noticed them, I can't help but see them everywhere I look.

A lightness spreads through my soul as I reminisce about a similar scene last year. I walked along this same path, the berries bright and pink evident all around me. Without careful observation, it was easy to focus only on dead and brown as I casually surveyed the scene, but when I slowed to notice, I couldn't help but find something beautiful and meaningful amongst the dormant foliage.

As I walk, I reflect on the summer and fall seasons leading up to this Christmas break. On the surface, life continued as normal—similar routines and patterns—but hardship churned beneath the surface. Many mornings I'd awaken with worry and fear gripping me over a heartbreaking challenge in our parenting season or a struggle at work. Darkness had a stronghold in our family in the last months, but through God's grace, we've begun to claw our way back to the Light. In the aftermath of each struggle, I was left feeling raw, weary, and far from living the abundant life..

I mentally tick through each circumstance and, with some surprise, begin to recognize each bright spot of Hope within the strife. A word of encouragement from a friend when hope seemed lost. An available appointment when darkness seemed to be closing in. A lighthearted moment when challenges seemed too heavy to bear. Soon, the words of a beloved Christmas song spring to life in my soul… "The thrill of hope, the weary world rejoices." I can almost hear my Hope whisper, "I have come that you might have life abundantly! You are no longer dormant; instead you are filled with the glory of abundant life!"

This season has been dark, like the night the angels declared Jesus' birth, but now as I walk along the neighborhood trail, it is suddenly ablaze with hope. Like the shepherds, I long to worship Him. For the remainder of my walk, my heart and soul echo the song of the heavenly host, "Glory to God in the highest!"

In John 10, John recounts Jesus, who was once worshiped by the shepherds of the field, calling himself a Good Shepherd, describing the difference between a shepherd leading his sheep and a thief coming in to destroy. Jesus teaches he has come to give life and give it to the fullest. He is the thrill of Hope. In the last months, the thief came to steal and destroy. But this morning, amidst the crimson red berries, I see evidence of our Hope. Our Good Shepherd is here, leading us toward life abundant.

— **Bethany McMillon**

Reflect & Respond

Where can we look for the beautiful signs of life He's given—life to be lived to the fullest?

NATURE

The third Sunday of Advent

On Sundays during Advent, we encourage you to gather with family and friends to enjoy fellowship and a time of encountering God together during the holiday season. (The devotion can also be done individually.)

During your time, you will be reading a reflection poem, discussing a few questions, participating in an optional exercise, and ending the time by lighting the third Advent candle, singing a song, and reading scripture. Make sure everything is ready before you begin.

Ask someone to read the Reflection out loud:

the gravity of sin
the weight of it holding nature down
holding down the trees
chaining mountains in place
the gray, cold darkness of an evil fog, deceitful
mist rolls from east to west
it stings the leaves and breaks off brittle trees
that used to pulse with joy
the earth itself dehydrated and full of deserts

cracking for lack of kingdom water
as the curse of corruption consumes the earth

the dull sound of drums
drowning out the gentle song of a billion stones
crying out in silent harmony
blessed be the King
blessed be the King
and the dust waits for the drums to still
the violence of man
blood soaking through it and pooling in
the center of the earth
and filling slowly, slowly til the earth's core
is full of the sounds of death and violence
calling for response
for justice
for an end to the futility, the bondage
it echoes through the canyons for all things
to be made right
to be made new

can you hear the lightning shout for justice
can you feel the earth tremble with barely suppressed rage
can you see the grasses sway across the open
plains as they moan for peace
and the mountains jut and jag and spike in
their attempt to break free
of the gravity of sin
they want to sway and bow down to the
throne as they used to
melodic voices gone mute but still they hum
too quiet for our ears

too quiet to be heard over the drums
no sound emerges but still they sing and shout
and roar and point
still the skies break each dawn and each dusk to proclaim
and the heavens tip over baskets of universes to declare
and the stars somersault across the sky to display
to pour forth night after night after night
of the glory, the glory, the glory

and they buckle from the weight of their desire to sing
but still they lift what they have
and they beg you to look and see in their beauty
who made them, who formed them,
who set them in their place
can you feel the beat in your chest of the earth itself
groaning for freedom
waiting, waiting
for the sons and daughters of God to be revealed

— **Jodi Cowles**

Questions for Discussion

1. Have you ever thought of what the earth looked like before Adam and Eve sinned? What might be different about creation when it is set free?

2. Psalm 19:1 says "The heavens declare the glory of God, and the sky above proclaims his handiwork." How do you see God in the heavens?

3. What do you think nature has to teach us as we all wait for the redemption of our bodies?

Optional Activity

Go outside for a few minutes (or moments, if it's 20 below) and select a piece of nature that stands out to you. Go back inside and warm up, then discuss what that piece of nature tells you about the nature of God.

Lighting the Advent Candle

Choose one person (a child if available) to light the third candle. Then ask someone to read the scriptures below.

Romans 8:18-23:

For I consider that the sufferings of this present time are not worth comparing with the glory that is to be revealed to us. For the creation waits with eager longing for the revealing of the sons of God. For the creation was subjected to futility, not willingly, but because of him who subjected it, in hope that the creation itself will be set free from its bondage to corruption and obtain the freedom of the glory of the children of God. For we know that the whole creation has been groaning together in the pains of childbirth until now. And not only the creation, but we ourselves, who have the firstfruits of the Spirit, groan inwardly as we wait eagerly for adoption as sons, the redemption of our bodies.

Sing a Song

Sing a song together! Whether you sing beautifully or badly, the point is to sing with abandon and joy in your heart.

O Holy Night

*O Holy Night, the stars are brightly shining;
It is the night of the dear Savior's birth;*

*Long lay the world in sin and error pining,
'Till He appeared and the soul felt its worth.*

*A thrill of hope the weary soul rejoices,
For yonder breaks a new and glorious morn;*

*Fall on your knees,
O hear the angel voices!
O night divine!
O night when Christ was born.
O night,
O holy night, O night divine.*

A thrill of hope the weary soul rejoices,
For yonder breaks a new and glorious morn;

Fall on your knees,
O hear the angel voices!
O night divine!
O night when Christ was born.
O night,
O holy night, O night divine.

Close in Prayer

Before your time comes to a close, take a few moments to pray for one another. These don't have to be long or eloquent prayers. But lift one another up by name before God. Ask for any specific prayer requests and allow time for everyone to pray who wants to pray. Ask for one person to close your prayer time.

SING

A world bent on darkness is now bathed in light. A Savior who draws near requires a response of praise.

As a people determined to worship, let us recalibrate our hearts back on the One truly deserving of our devotion.

Let us sing with our hearts, our bodies, our words, and actions as evidence of a resident Savior who is here with us and in us.

O come let us adore Him! Rejoice!

SING

week 4 – monday

*Love the Lord your God with all your heart and with all your
soul and with all your mind and with all your strength.*
Mark 12:30

I discovered the tuba as my calling in sixth grade. I started out wanting to be a percussionist in the middle school band, but so did every
other new band member, and I was plopped into the clarinet section.
A few weeks into school, my mom "accidentally" had not rented a
clarinet, and the band teacher was begging for a student or two to
switch to the tuba. Howling with laughter later that evening, my
mom (a clarinet hater) and I decided I might as well try out the heavy
instrument. I never would have expected that laughter-fueled switch
of instruments to set my life on a distinct and passion-filled path.

Happy with my switch to tuba, my middle school band director
inspired me to love music more than I ever expected. Band direc-
tors must be a special kind of people to realize their own calling
to music, pursue it their whole lives, and then decide they want
nothing more than to watch middle schoolers discover music. He

mentored me and helped me see I could glorify God by playing the tuba to the best of my ability.

Every day playing the tuba during my 6th-grade band class brought me joy. Though at first it sounded less like music and more like a whiny elephant, my band director was supportive and encouraging. I began to take pride in my talent and held myself to a high standard. I took my practice time very seriously, infatuated with the way the tuba's deep, rich sound filled the room. But I didn't know music could be its own path. All I saw was the middle school band.

During eighth grade, I was invited to participate in a middle school honors band in New York City and perform at Carnegie Hall. It was then I realized God could be directing me to pursue music through high school, into college, and beyond. As we started playing the music that we had come to know so well together, I was overwhelmed by the familiar warmth the tuba brings me. I listened across the musicians and back to my own beautiful sound and thought of all that I had learned in my pursuit to get there. I understood being at this stage was nowhere near the end of pursuing God's calling for me to use music to glorify Him, but just the beginning. It was thrilling and foundational to see I could pursue music professionally, and I celebrated the opportunity to pursue something I love for the glory of God by living out His calling on my life. That summer when I took my seat on the stage of Carnegie Hall with one hundred other wind musicians, I felt like I had "made it," as if my journey was ending.

I have begun to pursue music more seriously in high school through camps, additional bands outside of school, private lessons, and practicing (always practicing). Having a strong group of musical friends is essential for cultivating a strong sense of belonging, especially for young musicians. Glorifying God is easy when, together, my bandmates and I passionately engage in the creativity of music. I love the gleaming brass and deep, rich sound of the tuba. I love the smell of the metal and valve oil that rushes out when I open its case. I love hearing the clear, full, smooth sound as I fill the room with music. I love how I am enveloped in warmth as the room vibrates with its song.

God uses my love for the tuba to teach me to love others and Him with my whole being. My relationship with the tuba, music, and other people has brought deep joy to my life. When I read Mark 12:30, *"Love the Lord your God with all your heart and with all your soul and with all your mind and with all your strength,"* I think of the tuba. Through the immense joy I get when I play the tuba to the best of my ability, I know I'm loving God with my heart, soul, mind, and strength.

Every time I pick up my oversized instrument, I smile as I think about the experiences I've had over the past few years since the time my mom "forgot" to rent me a clarinet. I hope to continue the pursuit of glorifying God by playing the tuba for the rest of my life.

— Hollis Mitchell

Reflect & Respond

What are you passionate about?

How can you position that passion to bring glory to God?

SING

week 4 - tuesday

Let everything that has breath praise the Lord.
Psalm 150:6 (NIV)

One of my favorite things about Christmas is the myriad of songs that represent the holiday season. From crooning classics like "It's Beginning to Look a Lot Like Christmas" to peaceful hymns like "Silent Night," the songs we hear this festive time of year are too numerous to count.

No matter where you go in December, you can't help but hear Christmas music. There are radio stations that play Christmas music 24-7 from the day after Thanksgiving through midnight on Christmas Day. Every store you shop in has a Christmas playlist streaming through its sound system, and you typically have your choice of concerts or holiday shows if you prefer your Christmas music performed live and in person. Songs are everywhere at Christmas!

But singing at Christmas isn't something new. In fact, singing has been part of celebrating the birth of Christ since before Christ was even born.

Learning she would give birth to the Son of God, Mary sang praises to God, saying, *"Oh, how my soul praises the Lord. How my spirit rejoices in God my Savior! For he took notice of his lowly servant girl, and from now on all generations will call me blessed. For the Mighty One is holy, and he has done great things for me."* (Luke 1:46-49 NLT)

Zechariah praised God when he acknowledged the role his son, John, would play in preparing the way for Jesus, saying, *"And you, my little son, will be called the prophet of the Most High, because you will prepare the way for the Lord. You will tell his people how to find salvation through forgiveness of their sins. Because of God's tender mercy, the morning light from heaven is about to break upon us, to give light to those who sit in darkness and in the shadow of death, and to guide us to the path of peace."* (Luke 1:76-79)

The night Jesus was born, a host of angels praised God, singing, *"Glory to God in the highest heaven, and peace on earth to those with whom God is pleased!"* (Luke 2:14)

Simeon was an old man who loved God and had spent years praying and believing he would see the Messiah before his death. When Mary and Joseph brought baby Jesus to the temple to be circumcised, Simeon was there. Seeing baby Jesus, Simeon scooped Him into his arms and sang praises to God, saying, *"Sovereign Lord, now let your servant die in peace, as you have promised. I have seen your salvation, which you have prepared for all people. He is a light to reveal God to the nations, and he is the glory of all your people Israel!"* (Luke 2:29-32)

With hearts full of praise, these first witnesses couldn't help but sing songs of thanks for the gift of Jesus. They knew deep within their spirits that this baby was a miracle, an answer to generations and generations of prayers and prophecies.

When I think of the many things Jesus has done for me, I can't help but sing praises to Him. He has saved me, forgiven me, restored me to God, and given me the gift of eternal life with Him in heaven. He has blessed me with a beautiful family, wonderful friends, and caring and kind neighbors. He has healed deep hurts and helped to carry my worries and fears. He has gifted me with talents like writing and communicating to be a blessing to others and to bring glory to His name. He has been my truest friend, and He has never let me down. He has truly changed my life.

There are many reasons to sing praises at Christmas, but the greatest reason of all is Jesus. What praise will you offer Him today?

— **Leslee Stewart**

Reflect & Respond

What is your favorite Christmas song and why?

Reflect on a time someone praised you for a job well done. How did it make you feel?

Read Psalm 145 out loud. Does it feel different to say these verses out loud versus quietly reading them to yourself? If so, why?

Pick one verse from Psalm 145 that spoke to you. This week, try memorizing it to a familiar tune to help you commit it to memory and turn it into a song of praise.

SING

week 4 - wednesday

Sing to the Lord a new song; Sing to the Lord, all the earth.
Sing to the Lord, praise his name...
Psalm 96:1

The dimly lit sanctuary fills quickly. Large parties of friends and families slip into row after row. Small parties like our family of three fill in, and the occasional single person or couple slips in beside them all. We all hold small white candles, and an acoustic guitar strums "Away in a Manger."

Five trees line the back of the stage. White lights glow from their branches. As the lights dim, a hush falls over the crowd, and the musicians silently fill in around the guitarist to lead us in worship. One instrument plays quietly at first, then another, and another. Finally, voices raise the familiar notes of Christmas hymns, and the tunes swell around us.

Beside me sits my son, and beside him sits my husband. We stand together as the song begins. Like so many Christmas Eve services before, tears come quickly. I wipe them away, but soon my son's hand is in mine. He sings out "Joy to the World" in his teenage voice and I choke back more tears. I am overwhelmed with a sense of great peace and joy.

The music begins to carry me away to Christmases past. As a child, I traveled to my Gram and Grandpa's each year. Their home welcomed our entire family for festivities. Christmas Eve was a mound of gifts in front of an evergreen tree covered with multi-colored lights, and a huge dinner with laughter and a crescendo of noise just before we opened gifts. We often stayed for several days around Christmas, and within those days attended Sunday morning church. I fought for the chance to sit beside my Gram during the service; her voice singing the old hymns still echoes within my soul.

Years ago, just before we became a family of three, my husband and I imagined a quiet future of Christmas Eves and agreed we would always spend it at home and travel, if necessary, on Christmas Day. Once we moved away from our hometown, this indeed became our yearly rhythm. As our son grew, we held tight to our Christmas Eve service practice and added other yearly traditions, too—a family dinner, opening gifts after church, and a family picture by the tree.

For many years, the tempo of our Christmas Eves was light-hearted and fun, including the preparation of a plate of cookies for Santa and even a few treats for the reindeer and elves. But now, those traditions are changing. My son no longer reaches up to be held or climbs in my lap to tell me stories. Instead, his chin rests on the top of my head when he hugs me, and Christmas magic is only held in our memories. Instead of cookies for Santa, we opt for brownies, for all of us, and the pan of chocolatey goodness waits at home. Instead of packages of toys waiting under the tree, I've wrapped a few teen-approved gifts—books, gift cards, and some pajama pants with the logo of one of our favorite football teams. Tomorrow we will repeat our chorus of Christmas Day travel as we have for over a decade.

"Are you upset or are those happy tears?" His whispered question brings me back to the church service where we are. "Happy," I smile back. The splendor and majesty of our story, the allegro of our life is being written as we live.

The service continues with music, a dramatic retelling of the Christmas story, and a special message just for small children. My son is far too old to join the young ones for the story, but the memory is fresh of him timidly walking down the aisle to listen as our pastor spoke just to children.

Soon, the familiar chords of "Silent Night" fill the air, and one by one we pass a flame from candle to candle—through the crowd, finally to our row, first to my husband then to my son, finally to me. The voices of the congregation and the warm candlelight glow fill the sanctuary. My son holds his candle in one hand and reaches for my hand with the other. "All is calm, all is bright."

The teenage years are my new song, and I feel their rhythms accelerating quickly, before the decrescendo as he moves out from under our roof. The dynamics of our current music are still being composed.

In Psalm 96 David encourages us to sing a new song full of praise for all God has done. David acknowledges the greatness of God, and within each of these Christmas Eve memories, I rejoice before the Lord for Christmases past, present, and future.

— **Bethany McMillon**

Reflect & Respond

What new song is in your heart this year?

For what can you praise the name of the Lord?

SING

week 4 – thursday

Glory to God in the highest, and on earth peace among those with whom he is pleased!
Luke 2:13-14

When I was four years old, we lived in East Texas for a couple of years, prior to moving to Europe. One of the most special Christmas memories I have is of seeing, for the first time, a group of Christmas carolers. That Christmas Eve, I heard the wafting of melodic voices from somewhere down the street. I noticed that it seemed to get closer and closer, and then my father opened the front door.

A small group of neighbors stood before us, men, women, and children, well-worn music pages gripped between their fingers as they softly serenaded us with "Silent Night." Their eyes were lit with joy, tender smiles on their faces. I was mesmerized, frozen in a very special moment, though I didn't fully understand the magnitude of what they sang about. What I did understand was a feeling of connection to the music and the people as we stood before each other, some singing and some watching. We all seemed to comprehend that the song honored something, and some*one*, very special, and in that moment we were united in worship.

Christmas carols have the unique ability to touch the hearts of believers and nonbelievers alike. The songs carry a message of peace and love. They ignite a powerful joy within our spirits and serve as a reminder of Christ's birth, encouraging us to share the message of the hope found in Him. Singing is a spiritual language that can convey emotions, express spiritual truths, and even bridge the gaps between cultures and generations.

Have you ever noticed how all around the world, people seem to know the same Christmas hymns and carols, translated into their language of origin? Music is transcendent and unites people from all walks of life and even all stages of faith. "Silent Night," or "Stille Nacht," as it was originally written in German, was first performed on Christmas Eve, 1818, at the St. Nicholas parish church in a village in present-day Austria. Now, almost 200 years later, it is sung at Christmas time in over 300 languages. Transcendent.

Singing is significant to God. After all, He is the creator of sound, song, and emotion in the heavenly realms! The story of the Nativity reminds us of the impact made by song on the night of Christ's birth, when an angelic chorus filled the skies in Bethlehem, proclaiming the arrival of the Messiah. After telling the shepherds about the birth of Jesus, this angel was joined by an army of angels who sang praises to God, saying, "Glory to God in the highest, and on earth peace among those with whom he is pleased!" (Luke 2:13-14) The angels' song teaches us that singing is an expression of reverence, unceasing worship in the presence of God, and an understanding of the divine nature of that very moment in history.

Just as the angels sang together, we are also invited to join in the chorus of worship as the body of Christ. Throughout scripture, believers have used their voices to lift songs of praise up to God, acknowledging His eternal love, grace, and faithfulness. Singing alone allows us to engage our entire selves in a beautiful posture of melodic adoration, but singing with others in worship, whether a Christmas carol or a beloved old hymn, generates unity in the body of Christ. Just today, my pastor spoke on this very topic. Talk about God speaking through the spirit! He said when we worship with song, we engage with our God, interacting with Him as He interacts with us. When we join with fellow believers in worship, our voices meld harmoniously, bypassing our collective differences and creating a dulcet sound that is lifted to the heavens.

There is a beautiful worship song by Phil Wickham called "Reason I Sing" that ignites all my senses and illuminates the experience of worship. The lyrics of the chorus provide answers to the "why's" people may have when asking us about our belief in Him:

"For the cross that You bore, for the debt that You paid,
For the victory You won over death and the grave:
This is the reason I sing.
For the hope that you give, and the joy that you bring,
For the promise that heaven is waiting for me:
This is the reason I sing.[4]"

Earlier I shared a beloved childhood memory of watching carolers in front of our family home. A year after that, we left East Texas

4. Phil Wickham, "Reason I Sing," track 6 on *Hymn of Heaven*, Fair Trade Services and Columbia Records, 2021.

and moved overseas with my father's job. Once my brother and I left for college, my parents settled in England with my little sister. At that stage, Christmases meant traveling to our family home near Windsor to lament how dreary it can be across the pond when the sun sets at 4 p.m. in the winter months.

But there is one beautiful Christmas tradition I always looked forward to, that still makes me smile when I think about it. My father belongs to an old church in Beaconsfield called the United Reformed Church, whose history began in 1792 (the current building was built in 1874). Every Christmas Eve, the congregants gather on the front steps at midnight to sing centuries-old Christmas carols and hymns of worship. Never mind that the church steps face the rowdiest pub in town; the church secretary passes out the hymn sheets and the members of the Beaconsfield URC joyfully and boisterously sing out the likes of "Good King Wenceslas" and "Hark the Herald Angels Sing."

It doesn't matter that the congregation is tiny, or that the words are often sung off key, or even that sometimes the words aren't remembered. What matters are the people standing together, often in softly cascading snowfall, exchanging knowing smiles, pats on the shoulders from old friends, and the merriment and joy of the Christmas season.

— **Indee Musa**

Reflect & Respond

What is a Christmas song that makes you connect with the joy of the the season?

What is one reason you have to sing this Christmas? Take a few moments to thank God for His faithfulness and goodness in your life.

SING

week 4 - friday

For behold, the winter is past; the rain is over and gone. The flowers appear on the earth, the time of singing has come, and the voice of the turtledove is heard in our land.
Song of Songs 2:11-12 (ESV)

I used to think that the lovely birds who normally fill the sky and evergreen trees surrounding my home in the Cascade mountains all headed south when the snowflakes began to fly. As the branches and ground became blanketed with snow and ice, I no longer heard the welcoming chirps and melodious songs of my feathered companions, so I simply assumed they had all departed for warmer climates. That was until I noticed the steady visitation of winged friends enjoying my kind neighbor's daily buffet at his bird feeders. There were many little birds and larger birds alike. Sometimes, several varieties were perched on the feeders, partaking at the same time. Occasionally a bright blue and black Stellar's jay came swooping in to take command of the suet block, scattering the smaller birds. As the jays hammered away at the blocks with their strong beaks, filling up on large chunks, they sent a cascade of seeds to the ground. The little chickadees and nuthatches gratefully gathered the smaller bits into their hungry beaks before darting off to secure their treasures behind tree bark for a later date, remembering exactly where each cache was hidden.

I've since learned that while there are some birds who head to warmer climates, many stay behind with special adaptations to withstand the bitter-cold wind and snow of winter. They fluff their feathers to create spaces for trapping their body heat. They huddle together to share what little warmth they can create. They hunker down in tree crevices to avoid the breezes in between trips to their hidden storehouses, where they have stocked-up seeds gathered in preparation for these leaner times. Now that I know the birds are still out there, I watch for them darting in and out of swooping evergreen branches, just like they do in the warm summer months, but something is clearly missing. The forest is eerily silent during a calm winter snowfall and in between storms. The birds are still in the trees, but there are rarely songs to be heard. This is not a season for proclaiming territory or calling out for mates. No extra energy is spent on singing. They concentrate on survival in the cold winter months. They use their hard-earned calories to keep warm and out of reach of predators. Singing apparently needs to wait for another day. For now, they must consume enough food to simply stay warm until the temperatures rise again.

I have experienced seasons of "winter" in my life even when the weather was warm and sunny. Seasons of loneliness, isolation, illness, injury. Caring for loved ones who were in the midst of life changes they didn't want to make. Children who seemed to pass viruses back and forth. Forever. Computer "upgrades" at work that were nothing short of disastrous. Attending the funeral of a child. Singing was never on my mind during those times. Self-preservation was at the forefront. Just trying to make it through another day without crying was considered a success. A hot cup of tea offered by a co-worker was like my neighbor's bird feeder buffet. A text from a friend. A meal brought to my home. These were the offerings that kept me warm in the midst of the storms.

And then, one day in the forest, it happens. I hear it, and then I remember. A single note, more like a whistle, off in the distance. There is nothing more welcoming and stirring, as daylight arrives earlier each morning and lingers a little longer in the afternoon, than the sudden reappearance of that single note wafting on the breeze. I scan quickly in the direction of the note, coming from up high where the sun is reaching the droopy tips of the hemlock trees, and see a tiny bird that has begun to sing. Whether it's looking for a mate or proclaiming its place in the forest, I do not know, but for me, it is a song of welcome. Welcome to the sun. Welcome to the morning. Welcome to the promise of spring. Welcome to warmth.

Then another bird replies from a different treetop. Suddenly, a whole flock of birds swoops from one tree to another, all the while singing together, and a cacophony of music floods the once-silent forest. In the distance, there is the high whistle of the varied thrush meeting the song of another close by. Then my ears pick up the sound of the nuthatches joining in with their delicate chirping while clinging to the fir tree trunks. The hammering of the pileated woodpecker on a nearby snag, calling for a mate, is yet another piece of the percussion section in this beautiful forest symphony.

I still need my warm scarf and hat as the temperature hovers just above freezing, but these birds have endured much colder weather over these past months, so the longer sunlight and increased warmth are a blessing to be celebrated. They have stored up. They have remembered. They have huddled. They have adapted. They have endured. And now they celebrate a new season of life with song.

I experienced my own seasons of wintering while I guided my beloved mother-in-law through her final years. When I felt alone in making difficult decisions, God showed up in the wise advice and strong arms of a friend, repurposing furniture and possessions that held dear memories but needed to be released for someone else to enjoy. God showed up in the words of contemporary authors as well as ancient scriptures during times of illness that kept me housebound. God continues to show up in the beauty of nature and all her lessons when I feel isolated or alone.

— **Donna Dahlstrom**

Reflect & Respond

Since we all experience seasons of "winter" in our lives, times of hunkering down and just trying to stay warm, how do you adapt when a cold wind blows into your life? What resources do you rely upon in those challenging times?

week 4 - saturday

Jesus spoke to the people once more and said, "I am the light of the world. If you follow me, you won't have to walk in darkness, because you will have the light that leads to life."
John 8:12

The darkness, though unwelcome, wills us to sleep. In the dark, cold, and quiet, we shut off our minds and close our eyes. The darkness is a place of waiting for the light to break through. But when the long-awaited interruption comes, it can feel abrupt or unwanted.

I sleep with my windows open to let in a fresh breeze. At 4 a.m., when it is still dark out, the birds begin to sing in the middle of the night. It wakes me up, and although I want to go back to sleep, I cannot. These night songbirds sing in the darkness, announcing that dawn is coming even when it can't yet be seen. Their song, interrupting the dark, is an invitation to pay attention.

Mary, the mother of Jesus, personifies the singing songbird in the dark. She is a messenger of hope that comes in an unlikely package. The people of God were in darkness for 400 years, with each generation creating further distance from the stories of how God moved on the earth and delivered His people. They were waiting for the light to break in. But waiting is hard; over time, it lulled them into a sleepwalking state. Then, Mary—young, poor, and marginalized—arrived on the scene and started singing a song of faith and hope smack dab in the middle of intense darkness.

This song disrupted the darkness and the waiting, but for those not paying attention, it is easily missed. I've missed the gravity of Mary's song, sung in opposition to the weighty darkness that engulfed the Hebrew people for generations. If you've missed it too, let's not miss it now.

Read these words of Mary's song with a new understanding that she is the songbird singing prophetically in the darkness, proclaiming the light of the world that is coming and will soon arrive in the most unlikely of ways, the first being to occupy the womb of a young peasant virgin girl who is full of faith and responds with obedience.

"Oh, how my soul praises the Lord.
How my spirit rejoices in God my Savior!
For he took notice of his lowly servant girl,
and from now on all generations will call me blessed.
For the Mighty One is holy,
and he has done great things for me.
He shows mercy from generation to generation
to all who fear him.
His mighty arm has done tremendous things!
He has scattered the proud and haughty ones.
He has brought down princes from their thrones
and exalted the humble.

He has filled the hungry with good things
and sent the rich away with empty hands.
He has helped his servant Israel
and remembered to be merciful.
For he made this promise to our ancestors,
to Abraham and his children forever."
Luke 1:47-55

Mary and her people, the Israelites, were in the dark, waiting for the light of hope to break through. After Mary's visitation from the angel, she wondered, could this be? Mary was filled with hope but also doubt. She moved beyond the circle of her immediate family to find a place to process all that has happened and visits her older cousin, Elizabeth. Upon Mary's arrival and at the sound of her voice, the baby inside Elizabeth's womb leaps, and she is filled with the Holy Spirit. Elizabeth confirms in her words what the angel has spoken to Mary in secret. Mary rejoices as she realizes that the long-awaited light has come, and God has invited her to carry it in her womb. She opens her mouth at that moment, and Mary's song is released. The people are still in darkness, but she sings hoping that dawn will soon appear.

Today, not much has changed. We wait, yes, for Jesus' return, but like Mary, we wait with hope.

— **Connie Armerding**

Reflect & Respond

Can you hear the song of hope in the darkness? How is God asking you to be a messenger of hope, declaring the truth of His light?

The light of the world is coming—a light no darkness can overcome! Reflect on these scriptures of truth to build up your faith and confidence to declare the coming dawn, even when the darkness of the world and its circumstances surrounds you.

Isaiah 9:2
Isaiah 49:9
John 1:5
1 Peter 2:9

SING

The final Sunday of Advent

On Sundays during Advent, we encourage you to gather with family and friends to enjoy fellowship and a time of encountering God together during the holiday season. (The devotion can also be done individually.)

During your time, you will be reading a reflection poem, discussing a few questions, participating in an optional exercise, and ending the time by lighting the fourth Advent candle, singing a song, and reading scripture. Make sure everything is ready before you begin.

Ask someone to read the Reflection out loud:

in the middle of the deep green pastures
sing unto the Lord
in the middle of the desert, weary
sing
in the midst of deepest trial, deepest grief, and deepest pain
it's time to sing, to sing, to sing, to sing

at that moment you most gravely wonder what
the Lord is doing
sing a new song, write it if you must
when the tears don't stop from falling

for the joy that floods your soul you've got to
sing unto the Lord
and share your trust

when you're waiting for the water and you're
drowning in the dust
and you've persevered until your last, long breath
sing unto the Lord, cough it out into a whisper
make His praises oh-so-glorious

and when the water comes again as always it does come
and you are slaked and you are satisfied and full
sing louder of the One who knows exactly what you need
and to the worthy worthy worthy from your soul

sing about the good He's done, sing about His love unfolding
sing the overcoming of the Lamb
sing about the way He came into a manger lowly
six pounds, three ounces of the great I Am

sing about the story He is writing for us all
the greatest story we will tell for centuries
though it rarely goes the way that our most
fervent wishes plead
and we are often knocked about onto our knees

sing unto the Lord who comes exactly when He planned
who comes to overcome the evil and the lies
sing unto the One and join the song of all creation
heaven's thunderclap, a newborn's opened eyes

— **Jodi Cowles**

Questions for Discussion

1. What words would you have used if you were there when the baby Jesus opened up His eyes?

2. Can you each share one of the best things God has done for you this year and praise Him together?

3. What are some of the benefits of singing praise in the middle of difficult and challenging moments?

Optional Activity

Spend a few minutes writing your own psalms and share them with one another.

Lighting the Advent Candle

Choose one person (a child if available) to light the fourth candle. Then ask someone to read the scriptures below.

Read the following verses aloud

Psalm 23:1: The Lord is my shepherd. I lack nothing.

Psalm 98:1: Sing to the LORD a new song, for he has done marvelous things; his right hand and his holy arm have worked salvation for him.

Isaiah 9:6: For to us a child is born, to us a son is given; and the government shall be upon his shoulder, and his name shall be called Wonderful Counselor, Mighty God, Everlasting Father, Prince of Peace.

Sing a Song

Sing a song together! Whether you sing beautifully or badly, the point is to sing with abandon and joy in your heart.

Joy to the World

Joy to the world, the Lord is come
Let Earth receive her King
Let every heart prepare Him room
And Heaven and nature sing
And Heaven and nature sing
And Heaven, and Heaven, and nature sing

Joy to the Earth, the Savior reigns
Let all their songs employ
While fields and floods, rocks, hills and plains
Repeat the sounding joy
Repeat the sounding joy
Repeat, repeat, the sounding joy

He rules the world with truth and grace
And makes the nations prove
The glories of His righteousness
And wonders of His love
And wonders of His love
And wonders, wonders, of His love

Joy to the world, the Lord is come
Let Earth receive her King
Let every heart prepare Him room
And Heaven and nature sing
And Heaven and nature sing
And Heaven, and Heaven, and nature sing

Close in Prayer

Before your time comes to a close, take a few moments to pray for one another. These don't have to be long or eloquent prayers. But lift one another up by name before God. Ask for any specific prayer requests and allow time for everyone to pray who wants to pray. Ask for one person to close your prayer time.

Christmas Day

Merry Christmas! As you celebrate the end of Advent and welcome Christmas Day into your home, we encourage you to read the following passages from the Gospels that tell the story of Jesus's birth.

Mary's Good News
Luke 1:26-38

Joseph's Dream
Matthew 1:18-25

The Birth of Jesus
Luke 2:1-7

Shepherds Worship
Luke 2:8-20

Wise Men Worship
Matthew 2:1-12

Joseph's Warning
Matthew 2:13-23

Jesus is Our Salvation
John 3:16-17

An Epiphany on Epiphany

In 2017, skimming through the Biola University magazine, I was startled by a question in the final article: "Are you celebrating the holidays of your culture or of your faith?" *What do you mean?* I thought. *My faith is included in the holidays of my culture.*

Easter and Christmas were the only major holidays passed down to me through the centuries by my faith, and my childhood Christmas celebrations were fairly standard for an American Christian household. We always put up a Christmas tree and decorated with green and red. Mom and Dad skirted around Santa; while we five kids grew up knowing our gifts came from our parents, my dad would sometimes climb up on the roof and make Santa's sled tracks in the snow. As we grew up, our family added an annual Christmas shopping day in Lewiston, Idaho. We fanned out on Main Street to spend our own hard-earned-on-the-ranch dollars on a gift for each person in the family, meeting up for a sandwich, and dropping the occasional package beside the front tire of our family car for safe-keeping as we went past. Other than the shopping trips together, my going away to college didn't disrupt our traditions. For 71 years, I never once wondered, "What shall we do for Christmas?"

The author of the Biola article challenged me to consider the holidays of my faith, not just my culture. It brought back a half-forgotten memory: Through our Middle East Bible Lands tour business, my husband and I once brought a tour group to join hundreds of others from all over the world in observing Palm Sunday. Starting in Bethany, we all slowly walked down the steep and winding hill from the Mount of Olives past Gethsemane, on toward Jerusalem, entering the city through St. Stephen's Gate. Every group but ours was singing Palm Sunday songs in an incredible variety of languages. It was a thrill. Our group members walked, waved their palm branches, and gleefully took in the sights, but at the same time, we looked at each other in some dismay—because none of us knew a single Palm Sunday song.

Looking back on that experience, I began to wonder: What *were* the holidays of my faith? "From a handful of fishermen, tax collectors, and youthful troublemakers in an obscure province"[5], how have Christ-followers down through the centuries honored, celebrated, and remembered His birth?

In 1054, a thousand years of Christianity split into two large populations of Christians: Orthodox and Catholic. The Protestant Reformation in 1517 brought another split, and the splitting continues to this day. My history is Protestant, and as I began to research, it started to look like the Protestants—or my type, at least—had pretty much discarded everything but Easter and Christmas.

And yet, when you look in the Bible, it's easy to find evidence for the sanctity of celebration. God created the holy days and rituals detailed in our scriptures to help us know Him better and to assist us in remembering what He has done. For the Israelites, God initi-

5. https://christianhistoryinstitute.org/magazine/article/church-history-in-brief

ated annual celebrations to help them recall specific ways He had rescued them, like Passover for their delivery from Egypt and Purim as a reminder of Haman's defeat in Persia under Queen Esther. The Lord also instructed Joshua in how to remember the Jews' miraculous crossing of the Jordan River into the promised land, as we read in Joshua 4:3: *"Take up for yourselves twelve stones from the middle of the Jordan, right from where the priests stood.... because the waters of the Jordan were cut off before the ark of the covenant of the Lord... so these stones shall become a memorial for the sons of Israel forever."* God gave specific instructions about remembering via clothing in Numbers 15:38-40: He told the people to make tassels on the corners of their garments *"to look at and remember all the commands of the Lord, that you may obey them."* In Deuteronomy 6, we are instructed to use symbols and other means to recall God's commands. Communion was given to us for several reasons, including as a reminder: *"This is My body, which is for you; do this in remembrance of me"* (I Corinthians 11:24-28).

One of my favorite authors, the Nonconformist minister Matthew Henry, gave good advice in 1706, "The works of the Lord are so worthy of our remembrance, and the heart of man so prone to forget them, that various methods are needful to refresh our memories"[6]. Our history has proven that honoring holidays is one of the most persistent and effective of these methods.

---

6. https://www.christianity.com/bible/commentary/matthew-henry-concise/joshua/4#:~: text=Commentary%20on%20Joshua%204%3A1%2D9&text=The%20works%20 of%20the%20Lord,orders%20for%20preparing%20this%20memorial.

The Biola magazine article asked a question, and the Spirit guided me to an answer. Thankful for the Christians who have gone before, I chose over time to add to our family calendar the main holidays Catholics and the Orthodox traditions have in common: Advent, Epiphany, Lent, and Pentecost. By acknowledging these four holidays, I feel more connected to Jesus-followers around the world and through the centuries. But how do you start celebrating a holiday you know very little about?

Advent was easy: Our home church added an Advent celebration to the four Sundays of December many years ago. It was uplifting to watch friends and families with small children as they read the scriptures from the front of the church and lit the candles. Those services gave me the sense of a warm and fuzzy celebration.

I got a few more ideas in 2019 when I saw an advertisement for an Advent retreat at St. Gertrude's Monastery in Cottonwood, Idaho. After driving three or four hours through our beautiful mountains, my best friend and I checked in at the monastery for a three-day stay. The quiet and anticipation were palpable, mostly due to the tradition of silence between 9 p.m. and 9 a.m. It was startling to sit in a dining room full of people at breakfast, with no one speaking. Our retreat schedules were empty, only listing what was available. The monastery also demonstrated to us the practice of not decorating until Christmas Eve, and leaving the decorations up until Epiphany. It felt strange to be in a hotel-like environment in December with no Christmas decorations!

It also alerted me to how clueless I had been during all the years I worked a shift on Christmas Day as a nursing supervisor at a Catholic hospital. I had casually walked past an empty manager all that time, never noticing Jesus' absence, nor his Christmas Day appearance.

In reality, Advent, as a time of waiting, is a little bit dark and scary! An unwed mother conceives a child. That begins a period of heart-in-your-throat waiting. At some point her fiancé decides to stand with her instead of divorcing her quietly or exposing her to public disgrace—then, more waiting. Months of watching a pregnancy progress day-by-day in small-town Nazareth—waiting. Travel with a pregnant mom to Bethlehem, looking for a place to stay—that's an even more terrifying sort of waiting. Imagine preparing to give birth to your first child in a setting you never anticipated, without even a room to stay in! On a larger scale, the centuries of silence following the prophecies about Jesus had included massive amounts of waiting. Then, all at once, God came into our midst—God with us, Immanuel! Now it's Christmas!

But what comes after Christmas? Advent was already somewhat familiar, but I had to start from scratch learning about this holiday named Epiphany. The twelve days of Christmas were familiar to me only as song lyrics about leaping lords, calling birds, and partridges in a pear tree.

So I did some research. What came up was interesting to me, with the most clear explanation being the following:

"Epiphany is a festival in commemoration of the manifestation of Jesus Christ to the world as the Son of God, and refer[s] to the appearance of the star which announced our Saviour's birth to the Gentiles, and the visit of the Magi, or Wise Men of the East, to the infant Jesus. This festival is held on the 6th of January."[7]

For Christmas of 2021, we decided to celebrate Epiphany by inviting friends to a feast, commemorating the journey and arrival of the

---

7. Packer, George Nichols (1893). Our Calendar. Union and Advertiser Co. p. 110

Magi bringing gifts to the King. A delicious spread was enjoyed, and a take-out feast was delivered to quarantining friends! In the following years, along with the feast, we read aloud both the Biblical account of the star and the Magi and a children's book, *The Third Gift* by Linda Sue Park.

Looking back on the traditional Christmas celebrations of my past, I realize how much has changed. Celebrating Christmas for the period of December through Epiphany has caused a paradigm shift. My traditional Christmas celebration was tangled up with school programs and parties, work parties, open houses, additional responsibilities at church for the season, shopping, decorating, cooking, and extra cleaning in preparation for arriving family, topped off with the guilt of not celebrating Christ's birth "enough." Now, with a perspective change, December is Advent: waiting, anticipating, getting ready. On Christmas Eve we celebrate Christ's birth, and then we celebrate Emmanuel, God's presence with us, on through the 12 days of Christmas, experiencing a totally different kind of waiting.

The leadup to Epiphany, for me, is less of a time for anticipation and more of a blessed calm. *Ahhhh*. Reclining in my red lounge chair in the corner of our living room, I can look around our home with enjoyment. No plans spring into my head, just appreciation of what I can see: lights, music, decorations, Nativity sets, music boxes, a tree, and cards from those we love surrounding us like a warm blanket. I feel no anxiety, only gratitude to Jesus who came down to earth to save us.

The Magi were wise, so I like to imagine they, too, finished their Christmas journey with a sense of peace as well as anticipation. They had made a dangerous trip, but they had faith that they were being guided by a trustworthy hand. They must have known that, like everyone led forward by God's saving light, they would arrive exactly when they needed to, exactly where they needed to be.

If you would like to begin incorporating Epiphany into your family tradition, I would suggest the following:

- Keep your tree up for the 12 days following Christmas as a reminder.

- Now that the Christmas craze is passed, try to schedule fewer things during these 12 days so that you have time to reflect.

- Plan an Epiphany dinner on January 6th and invite friends and family to celebrate with you.

- Epiphany is sometimes called Three Kings Day, and celebrated by baking a "king's cake." If you have young children, they might enjoy the tradition of hiding a small trinket (often a little figurine of a baby) inside the cake. Whomever gets the slice of cake that has the trinket in it gets to be "king" for a day.

— **Jan Cowles**

ACKNOWLEDGMENTS

Thank you to each of the fantastic authors who worked hard writing these essays. Connie, Donna, Indee, Bethany, Hollis, and Jan, we are grateful for you! These were challenging essays with lofty subject matter, and we are so grateful for your contributions. Together, we made something beautiful and The Unknown Authors Club is thankful you have been a part of it.

We would also like to thank our summer intern, Paige Elliott for her brilliant editing, creative contributions, and thoughtful remarks on every aspect of this Advent project. We appreciate your willingness to jump in and add value to this book. We bragged about having a brilliant intern all summer and it felt accurate when you schooled us on dangling participles. We can't wait to see what lucky company will snatch you up after graduation. We consider you a long-term friend of The Unknown Authors Club. Best of luck!

— **Jodi Cowles, Rachael Mitchell & Leslee Stewart**
Founders
The Unknown Authors Club

ABOUT THE AUTHORS

CONNIE ARMERDING is a leadership coach and consultant, writer, speaker, and teacher. She is passionate about equipping ministry and marketplace leaders and their communities. Connie leads conflict resolution trainings for organizational teams around the Pacific Northwest. Connie's writing is published with Propel Women, Patheos, and the Redbud Post. She is a contributing writer of Friendzy, a K-8 school-wide social-emotional curriculum used in schools nationwide. She is a contributing writer for *Reflecting God's Nature,* the Women's Devotional Bible based on the Message. Connie has been married to the love of her life, Taylor, for twenty years, and they have four children.

DONNA DAHLSTROM can often be found wandering in the evergreen forest surrounding her home in the Cascade mountains east of Seattle, Washington. Her deep love of nature has opened her heart to the many spiritual lessons to be found in creation, among them rootedness, interconnection and reciprocity. Mother of three and Oma to four adventuresome granddaughters, connecting young moms with seasoned mentors has been her passion for over two decades. She is the author of *Harriet's Grand Discovery*, joining her appreciation of the unique adaptations of the snowshoe hare while celebrating the special qualities that each individual brings to our world. She enjoys hiking and skiing alongside her fellow author and husband, Richard, as well as guiding interpretive snowshoe treks for children and adults alike.

JAN COWLES was raised on an Idaho ranch, learning early the value of family and hard work. She went on to earn her degree as part of the first baccalaureate nursing class at Biola University, then joined the army and, and instead of receiving an honorable discharge, sewed her own maternity uniform in order to continue serving. She flew on Huey helicopters over northern Germany as a public health nurse, before retiring from the Army and beginning a new, 30-year career as a nursing administrator in Boise, Idaho. Jan joined her husband of more than 50 years, Tim, in their travel business, taking groups to the Holy Lands of Israel, Jordan, Egypt, Turkey and Greece for 37 years. Additionally, her lifelong passion for global outreach has had her "volunteering" in various positions over the years. Jan is a happy gramma, loves moving water, and is a prolific reader.

JODI COWLES is an American author who spent eight years living (and mostly loving) life with her husband and daughter in Istanbul, Turkey. Spending more than half her adult life living and working in seven different countries, her time abroad expanded her vision of the world and allowed her to collect stories along the way. Armed with an endless supply of culture-clashing mishaps, inappropriate marriage proposals, and language barrier misfires, Jodi's writing gets to the heart of the matter: the human connection present in every country and culture. Her most recent novel, *Cold Turkey*, is a humorous romp through the colorful and crowded chaos of life as a foreigner in Turkey. You can find out more at www.jodicowles.com or on Instagram @jodicowles.

BETHANY MCMILLON is a coffee, football, and ice cream lover from Texas. She adores her number-loving accountant husband and her too-close-to-grown boy. Bethany loves her work as an assistant principal, and she is passionate about building deeper relationships with both Jesus and those that she loves. Her spirit is most settled after she has connected with a friend about God's mercy and grace over coffee, sweet tea, or even a side-by-side walk through a local neighborhood. She hopes to encourage women to find and hold onto those connections within busy and quick-paced lives. Bethany is a contributing author in two books (so far!): *Strong, Brave and Beautiful: Stories of Hope for Moms in the Weeds*, an anthology written by Emily Allen and members of the Kindred Mom team, and *The Life of an Unknown Author: An Anthology on Writing and Publishing from Some of the Best Authors You Haven't Yet Read.* You can find more at www.BethanyMcMillon.com or on Instagram @ BethanyMcMillon.

HOLLIS MITCHELL is a sophomore at Issaquah High School who plays her tuba in four bands and one orchestra. She doesn't have free time, but somehow fits in playing on the school's frisbee team, drivers ed, and homework. She shares a devout love of nature in addition to the tuba. When the stars align, and she has a quiet afternoon with no obligations, you'll find Hollis hunting for honey bee habitats in the wild. She has traveled to Alaska the last four summers to salmon fish with her dad and best friend and she secretly aspires to quit high school and join a traveling brass band (but don't tell her parents!).

RACHAEL MITCHELL is a writer and speaker, wife and mom, who relies on faith, humor and an up-to-date Google calendar to make it through the day. There's a high chance you'll catch Rachael dressed in sweatpants with a book in one hand, a cup of tea in the other, totally forgetting that she's supposed to be in the car picking up a kid from soccer practice. She majored in English, was a paid product copywriter for two large national retailers, and launched Mitchell Freelance in 2020. Her copywriting business provides well-known and mom-and-pop companies strong, but clear and concise copy. With all the writing she's done for everyone else, it was high time she wrote for herself. Rachael and two friends, also fellow writers, launched The Unknown Authors Club, a platform to discover and amplify the untapped voices of other unknown authors with tiny platforms and big stories. Rachael enjoys the beach, connecting with friends and family, and resides in Issaquah, WA. For more, visit www.rachaelmitchell.com.

INDEE MUSA grew up an ex-pat kid, traveling between India, Lebanon, Greece, and eventually East Texas. Raised by Lebanese parents, her childhood was filled with the love of the culture of her country of origin, Lebanon, as well as a passion for seeing the world. Indee has always loved reading and writing, and growing up she could often be found in the basement bookstore of the American Club in Athens, lap filled with books by Erma Bombeck, Judy Blume, and Archie comics. Indee's journey into adulthood took her down some n'er trodden paths but eventually her renewed faith spit her back out on the right one. Never mind it was the long route.

While her family remains scattered worldwide, she treasures moments with them, her dear friends, and her college-aged daughter. She's currently penning a memoir about her faith journey as a single mother and still dreams about Lorne Michaels casting her on *Saturday Night Live*. For more, visit www.indeemusa.com.

LESLEE STEWART began her career as a newspaper reporter, and spent the next two decades leading communications for some of the best-known brands in the world, including Victoria's Secret. Today, she encourages others through speaking engagements, writing, and helping undiscovered authors get published through The Unknowns Authors Club. And when she's not doing those things, she's usually sitting in the bleachers next to her husband, cheering on their two, sports-obsessed teenage sons. Her goals in life are simple — learning to master the perfect guacamole, getting her boys to appreciate musicals, and someday singing backup for Aretha Franklin in heaven. Her debut book of essays on the funny, fearful, and unforgettable moments of life, *A Little Bit About a Lot of Things*, was released in early 2023. For more, visit www.lesleestewart.com.

ABOUT THE UNKNOWN
AUTHORS CLUB

THE UNKNOWN AUTHORS CLUB was formed by Jodi Cowles, Rachael Mitchell, and Leslee Stewart—three aspiring authors who met in a writing cohort in March 2021. Each arrived at the cohort with a book in their heart and a dream of being courted by a publisher who would bring their book ideas to life. But those dreams were quickly dashed after each submitted their proposals and received a chorus of resounding "no's" from publishers. The problem wasn't their content—these three could definitely write! The problem was nobody knew who they were. No publisher would take a chance on a writer who didn't have a built-in audience of tens of thousands of potential readers.

Disappointed but determined, these three set out to find a new way to help authors like themselves get published, even if they're not currently trending on TikTok. Together, they created a social community and publishing company designed to celebrate unknown authors regardless of their influencer status.

Their first publication, *The Life of an Unknown Author: an Anthology on Writing and Publishing from the Best Authors You Haven't Yet Read* features essays from the three founders, as well as fellow unknown authors, all focused on the topic of what it means to be unknown.

Other titles under their imprint include *A Little Bit About a Lot of Things: Finding Freedom in the Funny, Fearful, and Unforgettable Moments of Life* by Leslee Stewart, *Cold Turkey* by Jodi Cowles, and *Covered: My Breast Cancer Story and Practical Insight for Yours* by Tanya Motorin.

To find out more, visit theunknownauthorsclub.com or follow their adventures on Instagram @theunknownauthorsclub.

HERE ARE SOME EASY WAYS TO SUPPORT THIS BOOK

 Share a picture of the book and tag @theunknownauthorsclub

 Leave a review on Amazon or Goodreads

 Buy a copy as a gift

 Tell a friend about the book

 Ask your local bookstore to carry it

theunknownauthorsclub.com

Made in United States
Orlando, FL
08 December 2023

40408090R00107